Welcome to the
Plus Up Phonics Series!

Author **Joy Park**
Supervisor **LittleLambSchool**
English Research Institute

Author : Joy Park

Welcome to the "Plus Up Phonics Series!
Studying English phonics is necessary for learning English. But we usually think that it is not that easy to learn and even sometimes boring. Yes, right. In terms of this view, I tried to focus on stimulating English learners not to run away from learning English phonics.
Plus Up Phonics contains all of the basic and essential parts for learning English phonics and of course, it consists of many exciting and practical activities for learners.
I hope Plus Up Phonics will help your students have great confidence in English Phonics.

Supervisor : LittleLambSchool English Research Institute

"Plus Up Phonics" has everything your English learners need to begin their first step in English phonics. Because Plus Up Phonics is made of interesting word games and various phonics questions, students cannot lose their concentration on learning English phonics and also it will give a balanced knowledge of essential parts of English phonics.
We hope your students could get off on the right foot in English with the Plus Up Phonics!

About the Book

How to use Plus Up Phonics

Plus Up Phonics will allow your students to take their first right step in English.
Here are some suggestions to get the most out of this book.
Each lesson provides time allotment and homework check box for the effective and practical teaching.

Consists of Each Unit

❶ Listen and Repeat: My Dictionary
Students listen to and reproduce the sounds they hear in words.
Also while they find words they hear in the book, they can maintain their interests in phonics.

❷ Presentation: Short-Story, Chant, Odd Poem, and Song
Students can look around words based on English phonics learned through four various kinds of writings: story, chant, poem and song.

❸ Let's Practice Phonics: Phonics Listening
Students can check their understandings based on English phonics learned carefully by solving the listening questions.

❹ Pop Quiz & Mini Test
Check the weak points and review each unit briefly.

❺ Let's Play: Phonics Activity
Through the interesting English phonics word games, students can practice in a natural way.

❻ Homework Spot
Homework Spot contains three kinds of phonics questions: listening, reading and writing questions. These will help your students wrap up each unit in detail.

CONTENTS

Listen and repeat. Track 01

Aa Bb Cc Dd Ee Ff Gg Hh Ii Jj Kk Ll Mm
Nn Oo Pp Qq Rr Ss Tt Uu Vv Ww Xx Yy Zz

Trace the uppercase letters.

A B C D E

Trace the lowercase letters.

a b c

Write the uppercase and lowercase letters.

 ill in the blanks.

A	b	c	D	E
F	G	h	I	j
K	L	m	n	o
P	Q	r	S	T
U	v	w	X	Y
Z				

C omplete the chart.

Vowels	Consonants

The Letters and Sounds **Aa, Ee, Ii**

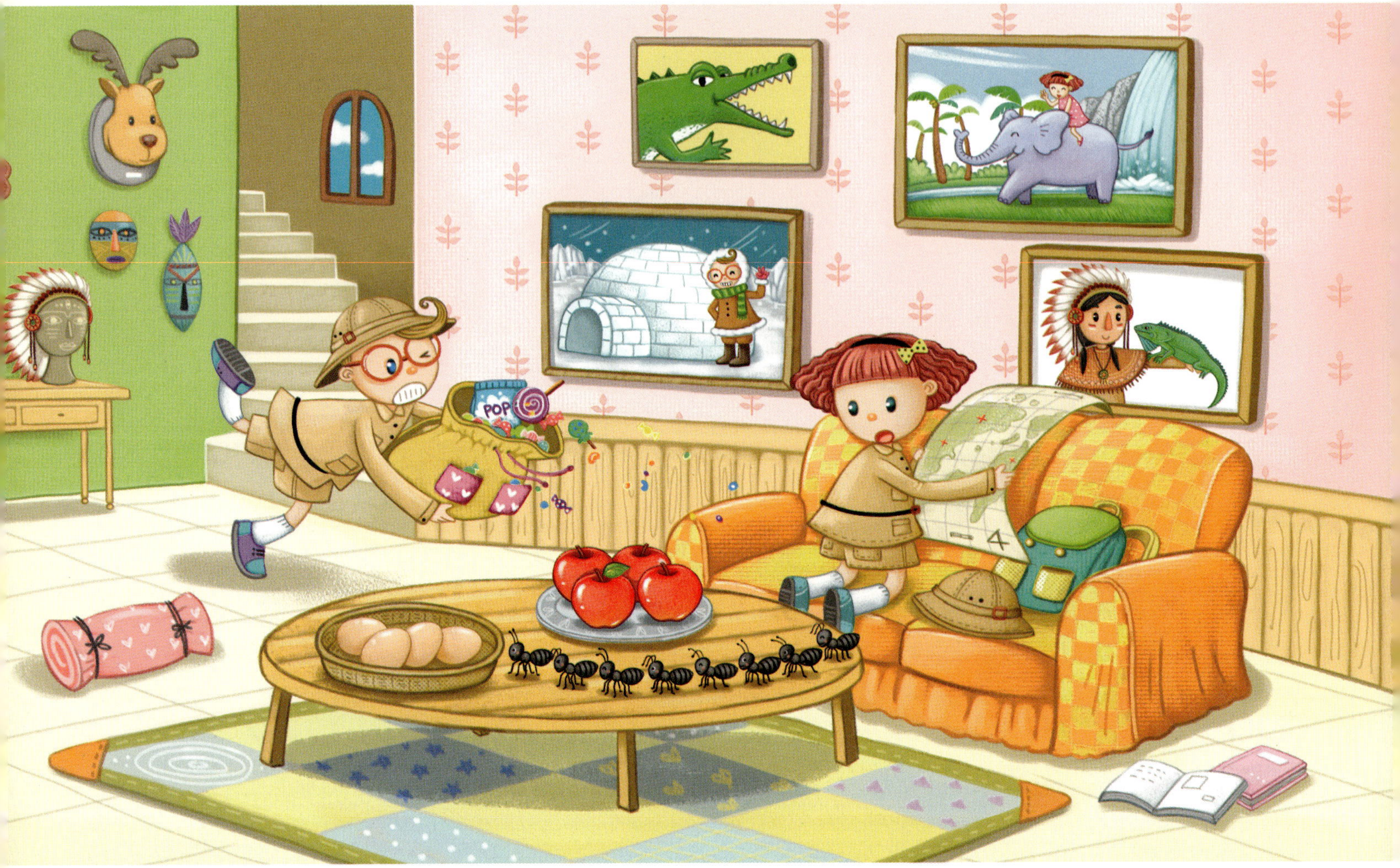

Look and find the new word, then circle.

Listen, repeat and check.　Track 02

ant	☐	eight	☐
apple	☐	igloo	☐
alligator	☐	Indian	☐
egg	☐	iguana	☐
elephant	☐		

My Dictionary

Read and write.

A A a a

E E e e

I I i i

 Let's Chant  10min

L isten and repeat. Track 03

A - a - a says /a/ /a/  apple.

A - a - a says /a/ /a/  alligator.

The alligator says, "Apples are good."

E - e - e says /e/ /e/  elephant.

E - e - e says /e/ /e/  egg.

The elephant says, "Eight eggs."

I - i - i says /i/ /i/ Indian.

I - i - i says /i/ /i/ igloo.

The Indian says, "A cold igloo."

Aa
Ee
Ii

 Write the beginning letter.

1.  _______

2.  _______

3.  _______

4.  8 _______

5.  _______

6.  _______

7.  _______

8.  _______

Listen and circle the correct beginning letter. `Track 04`

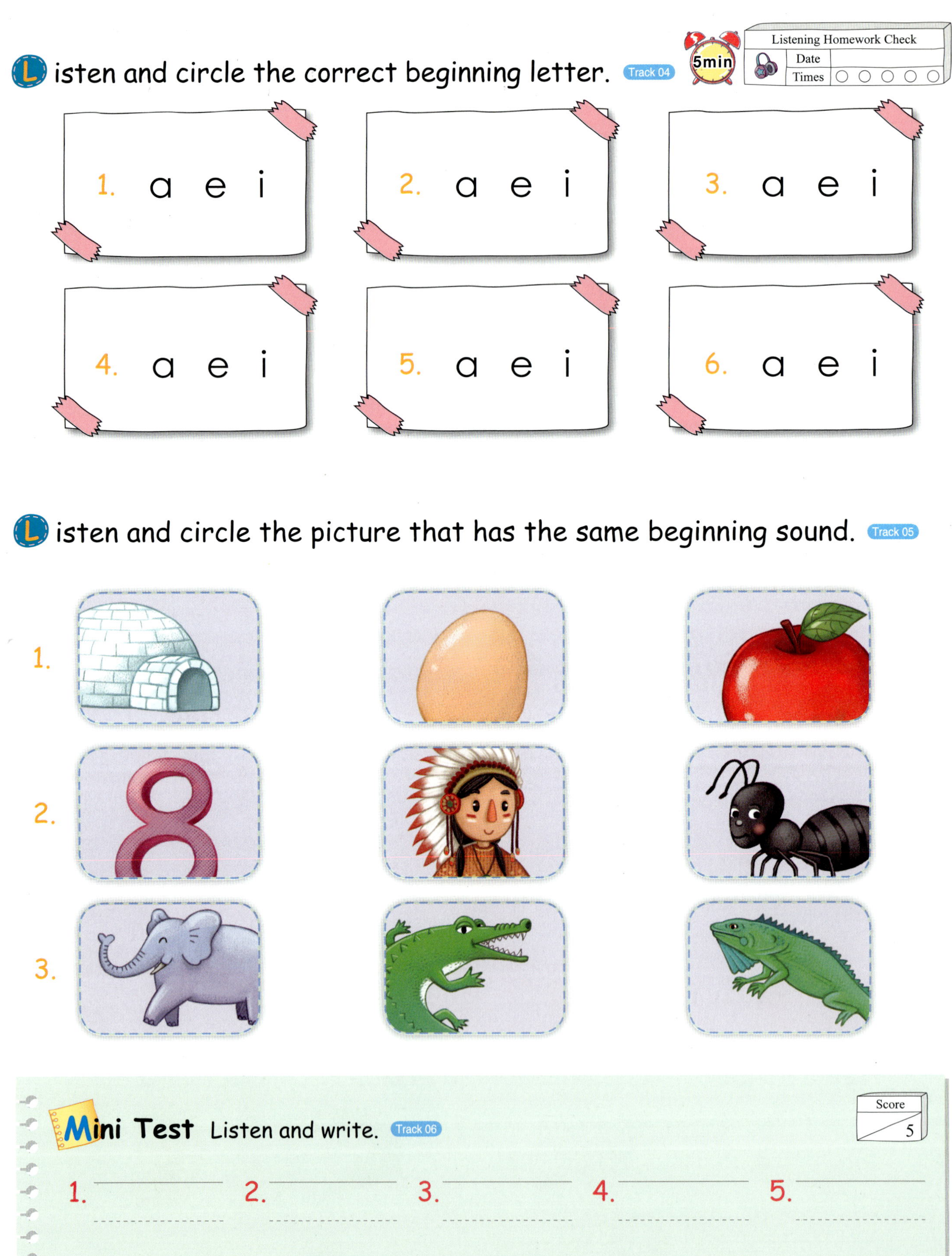

1. a e i

2. a e i

3. a e i

4. a e i

5. a e i

6. a e i

Listen and circle the picture that has the same beginning sound. `Track 05`

1.

2.

3.

Mini Test Listen and write. `Track 06`

Score / 5

1. _____ 2. _____ 3. _____ 4. _____ 5. _____

Look and circle the correct word.

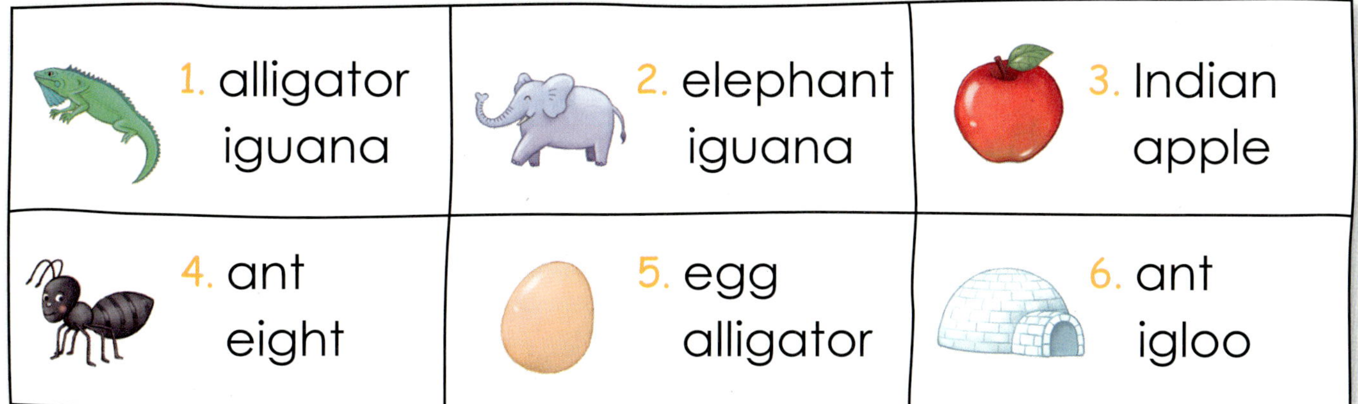

1. alligator / iguana	2. elephant / iguana	3. Indian / apple
4. ant / eight	5. egg / alligator	6. ant / igloo

Read and trace.

A red apple.
A yellow elephant.
The eight ants and eggs.
An alligator and an Indian.

Hunting Letters

15min

| Dice | Markers |

How to play

❶ 각 빈칸에 알파벳의 짝 글자를 쓰게 합니다.

❷ 주사위를 던져 도착한 칸의 알파벳의 소리를 말하게 하고 그림 칸에서는 그림의 단어와 첫소리 알파벳을 말하면서 전진해 가장 먼저 도착한 사람이 승리의 얼굴에 색칠합니다.

❸ 게임은 수업시간에 따라 1회 또는 2회를 합니다. 가정에서도 게임숙제를 하고 그 결과에 따라 얼굴을 색칠하게 합니다.

	1st round	2nd round
In the class		
At home		

Track 07

1 Listen and choose the correct letter.

❶ Aa   Ee   Ii   ❷ Aa   Ee   Ii   ❸ Aa   Ee   Ii

❹ Aa   Ee   Ii   ❺ Aa   Ee   Ii   ❻ Aa   Ee   Ii

2 Listen and write the letter in order.

❶ ◯ → ❷ ◯ → ❸ ◯ → ❹ ◯

3 Listen and circle the picture.

A - a - a says /a/ /a/ 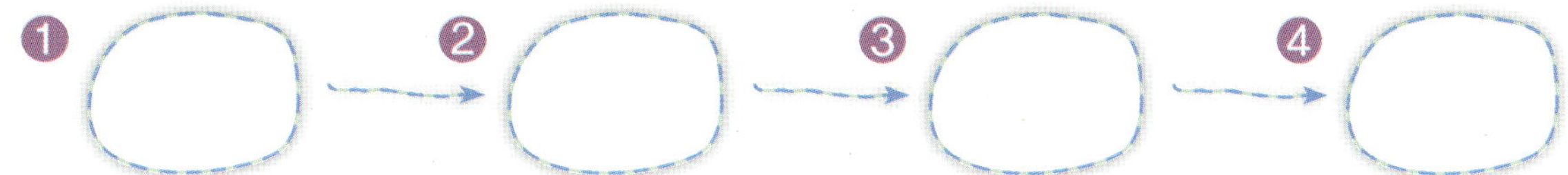 .

The alligator  says, "Apples are good."

E - e - e says /e/ /e/  .

The elephant  says, "Eight eggs."

I - i - i says /i/ /i/  .

The Indian  says, "A cold igloo."

4 Look, listen and circle.

The Letters and Sounds Oo, Uu

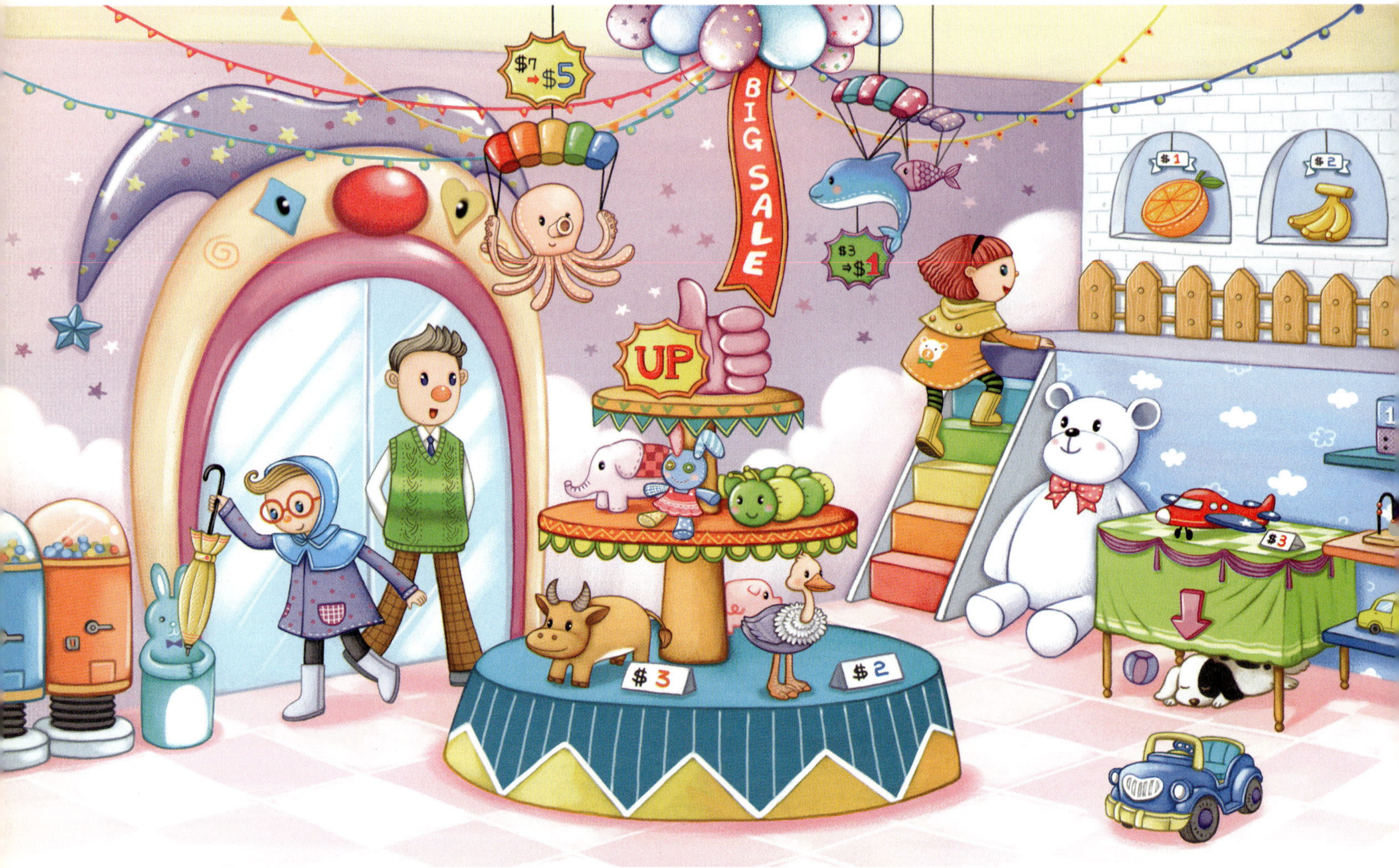

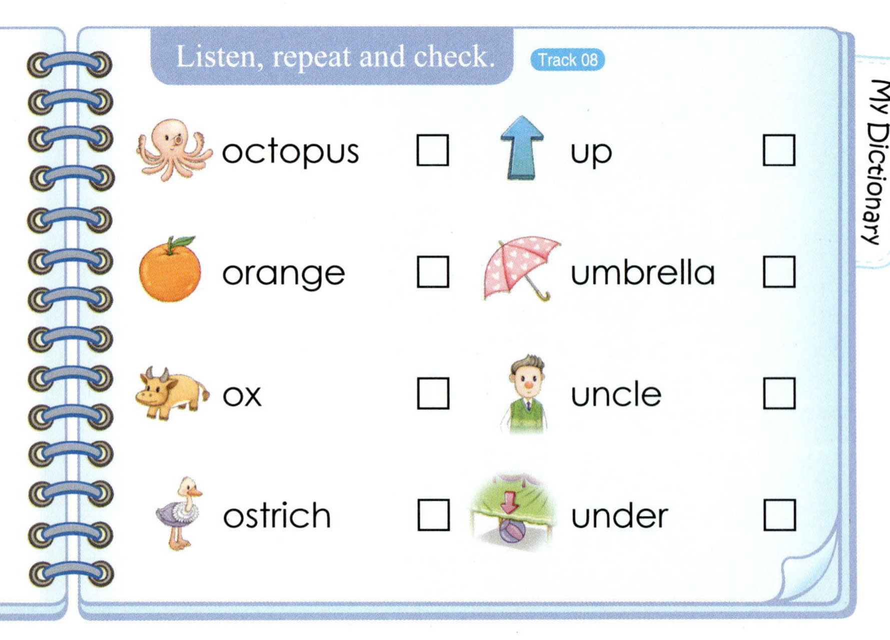

Look and find the new word, then circle.

Listen, repeat and check. Track 08

- octopus ☐
- up ☐
- orange ☐
- umbrella ☐
- ox ☐
- uncle ☐
- ostrich ☐
- under ☐

My Dictionary

Read and write.

O O O

U U U

O O O   U U U

 Let's Chant

10min

L isten and repeat. *Track 09*

O - o - o says /o/ /o/  orange.
O - o - o says /o/ /o/  octopus.
O - o - o says /o/ /o/ ostrich.

The ostrich and

the octopus like oranges.

U - u - u says /u/ /u/  umbrella.
U - u - u says /u/ /u/  under.
U - u - u says /u/ /u/  uncle.

Look at my uncle.

He is under the umbrella.

Oo
Uu

POP QUIZ — Write the beginning letter.

Score / 8

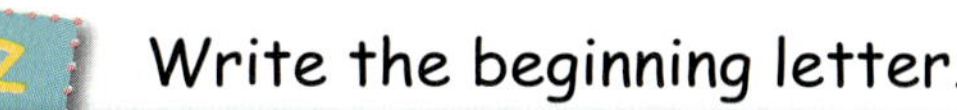

1.    2.    3.    4. 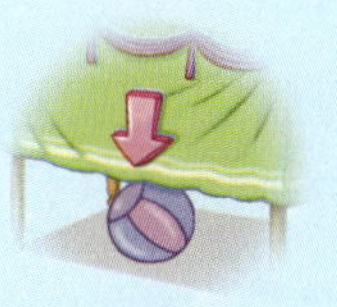

__________   __________   __________   __________

5.    6.    7.    8. 

__________   __________   __________   __________

Listen and circle "Yes" if both have the same beginning sound or "No" if not. Track 10

1. Yes No	2. Yes No	3. Yes No
4. Yes No	5. Yes No	6. Yes No

Listen and match the picture to the bowling pin. Track 11

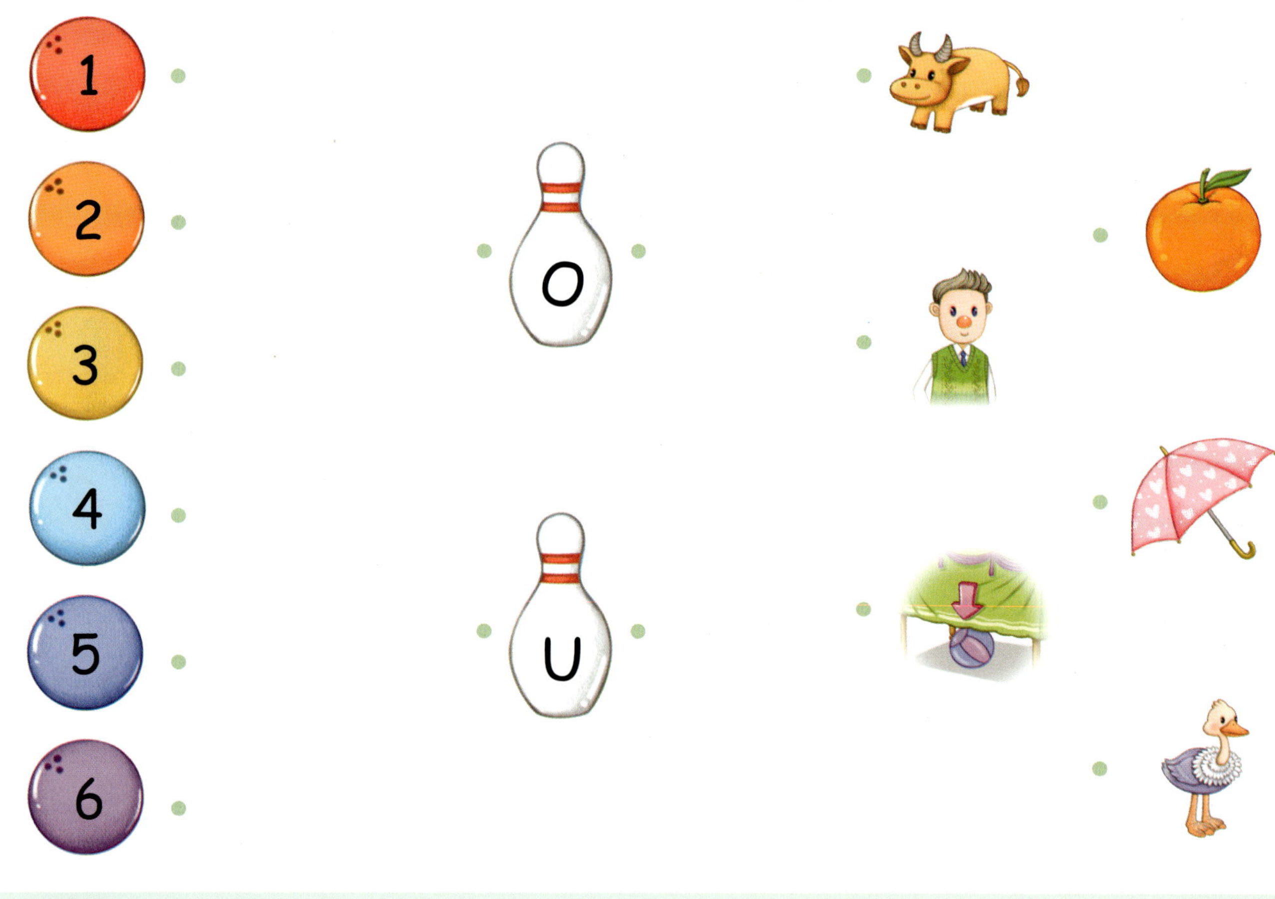

Mini Test Listen and write. Track 12

Score
/5

1. _______ 2. _______ 3. _______ 4. _______ 5. _______

F ill in the circle next to the correct beginning letter sound for each picture.

1.  a ○ o ○ u ○

2.  a ○ e ○ i ○

3. a ○ o ○ u ○

4. a ○ e ○ i ○ o ○

5. a ○ o ○ u ○

6. a ○ i ○ u ○

7.  e ○ i ○ u ○

8. i ○ o ○ u ○

9. 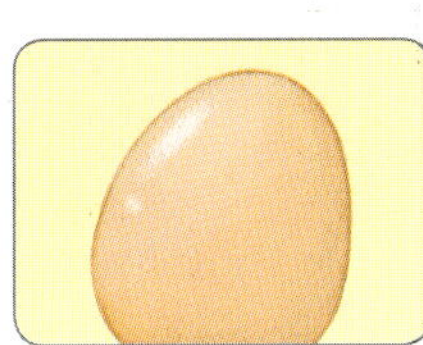 a ○ e ○ i ○

Oo Uu

L ook and fill in the blanks from the word box. Then listen. Track 13

The ____________ is under the table.

The ____________ is under the hat.

The ____________ is under the umbrella.

"Happy birthday"

____________ John.

Here some ____________ .

Word Box   ox oranges ostrich octopus uncle

Let's Play

Bingo

15min

How to play

❶ 빙고게임을 하기 전에 각 그림 아래 동그라미에 첫소리 글자를 모두 적으며 모음전체를 복습합니다.
❷ 빙고 1은 a, e, i 를 빙고 2는 o u 를 빙고 3은 a, e, i, o, u 전체(대문자, 소문자로 구분해서)를 게임을 통해 복습합니다.
❸ 각 빙고 칸을 지울 때 반드시 알파벳의 첫소리 또는 그 첫소리를 가진 단어를 말해야만 지울 수 있게 합니다.

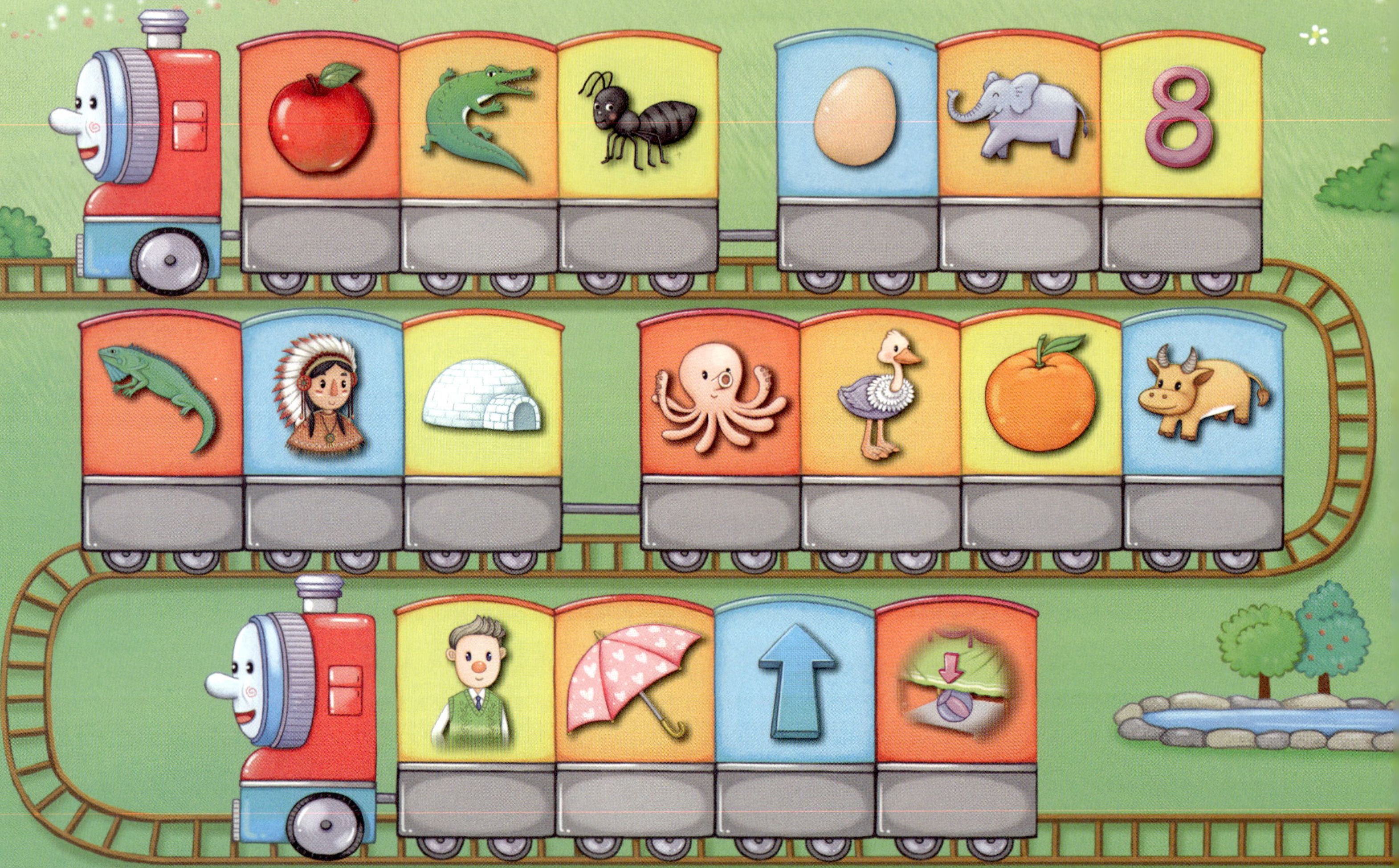

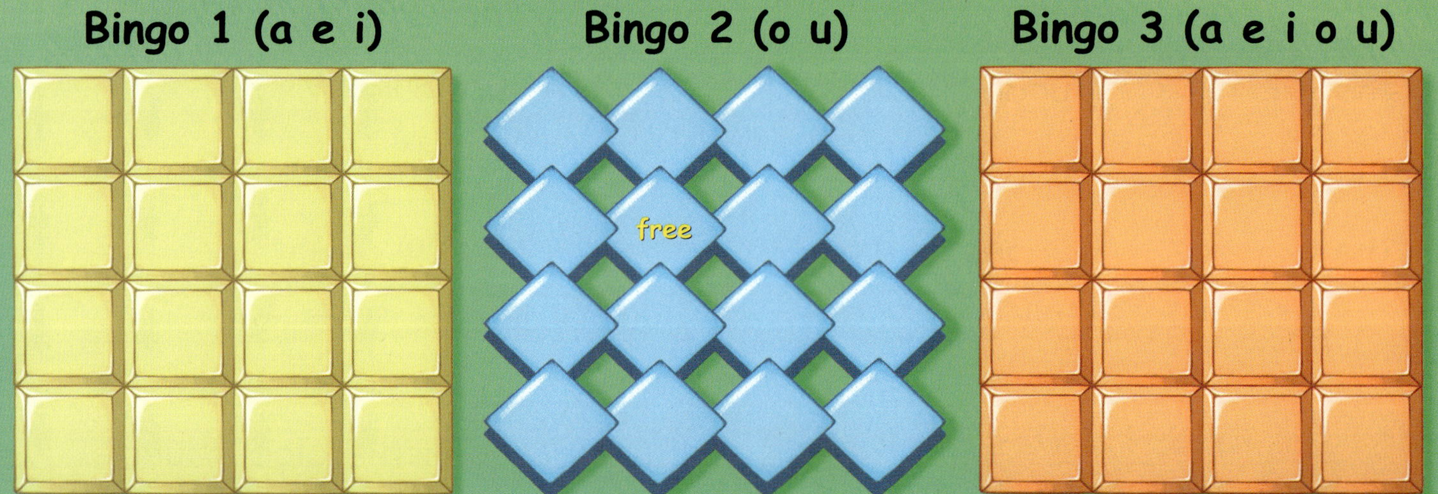

Bingo 1 (a e i)

Bingo 2 (o u)

Bingo 3 (a e i o u)

Track 14

1 Listen and circle the same beginning sound.

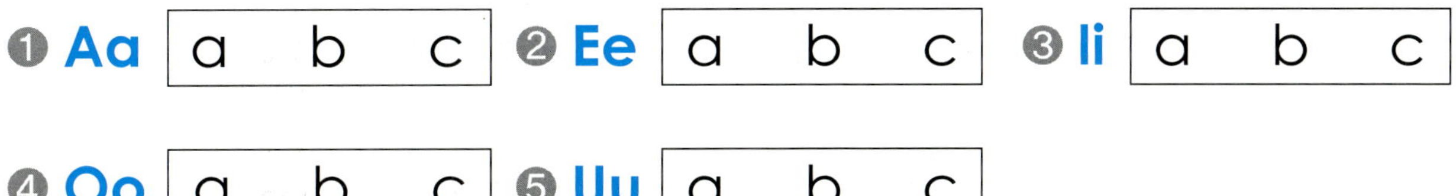

2 Listen and write the beginning letter.

3 Listen and circle the correct word.

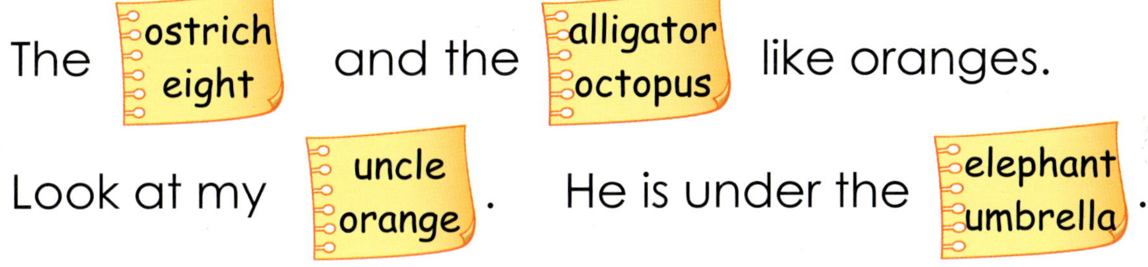

4 Look, listen and circle.

The Letters and Sounds Bb, Cc, Dd, Ff

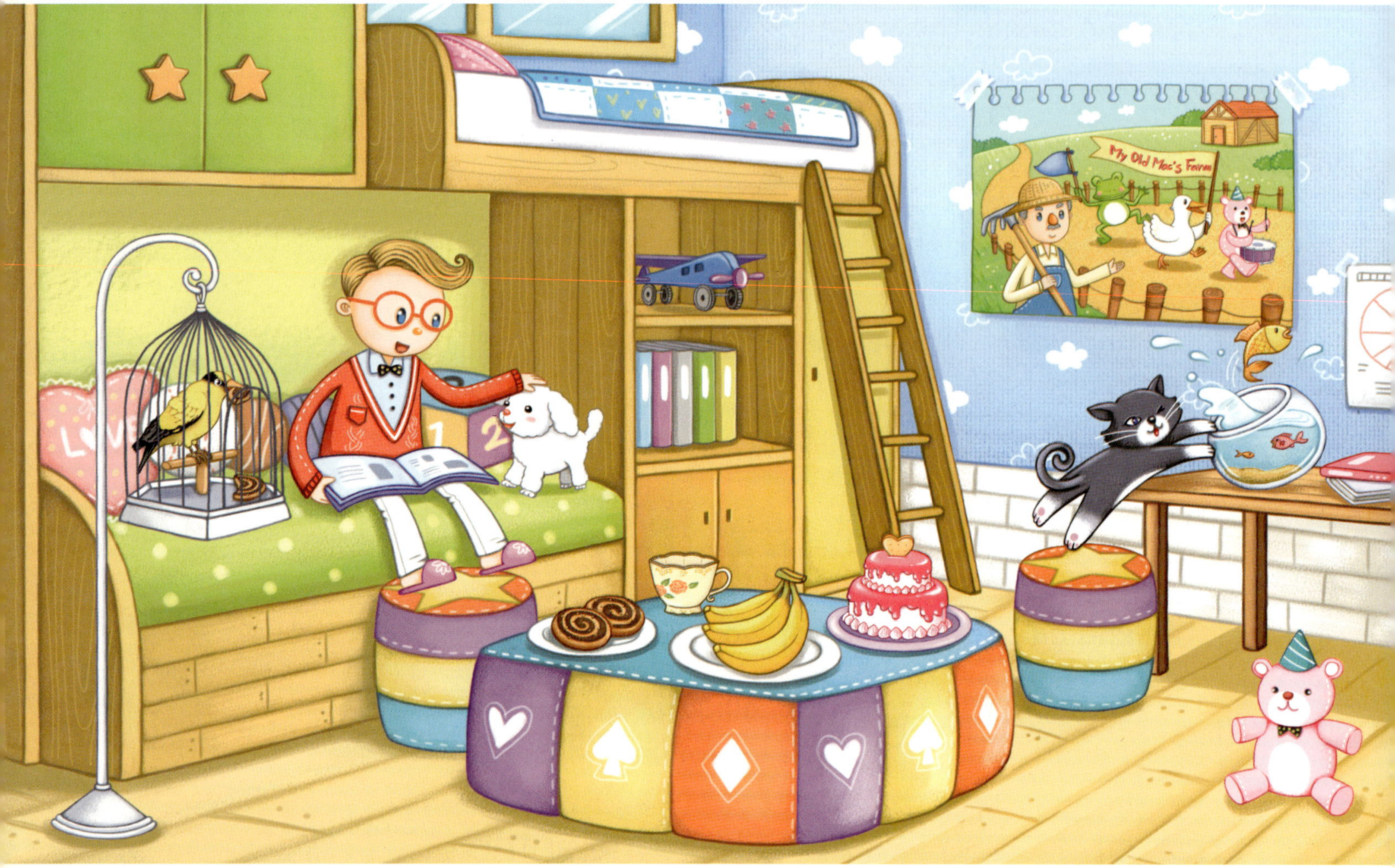

Look and find the new word, then circle.

Listen, repeat and check. Track 15

boy	☐	dog	☐	
banana	☐	duck	☐	
bird	☐	drum	☐	
book	☐	doll	☐	
cat	☐	fish	☐	
cup	☐	frog	☐	
cookie	☐	flag	☐	
cake	☐	farmer	☐	

My Dictionary

Read and write.

B B b b

C C c c

D D d d

F F f f

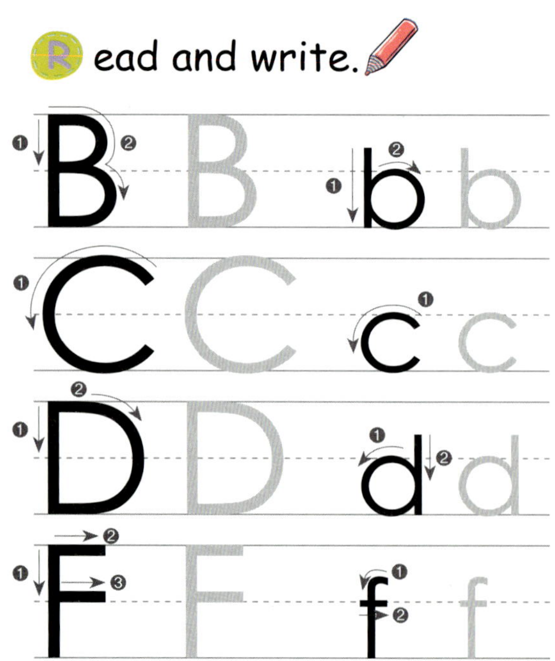

18

10min

L isten and circle. Then repeat. Track 16

B - b - b says /b/ /b/  .
B - b - b says /b/ /b/ .
C - c - c says /c/ /c/ .
C - c - c says /c/ /c/ .

The bird on the book. Cookies on the cake.

D - d - d says /d/ /d/  .
D - d - d says /d/ /d/ .
F - f - f says /f/ /f/ .
F - f - f says /f/ /f/ .

The dog has a drum. The farmer has fish.

POP QUIZ Write the beginning letter.

Score
8

1. _______ 2. _______ 3. _______ 4. _______

5. _______ 6. _______ 7. _______ 8. _______

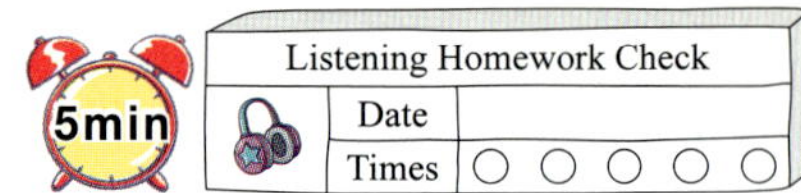

Listen and circle the correct picture. Track 17

1. 

2. 

3. 

4. 

5. 

6. 

isten and write the missing letter. Draw a line to the picture. Track 18

1. ☐at   2. ☐armer   3. ☐oll   4. ☐oy

Mini Test Listen and write. Track 19

1. _______   2. _______   3. _______   4. _______   5. _______

20

Read the letter and Put an "X" on the picture that has different beginning sound.

Bb | Cc | Dd | Ff

Read and fill in the blanks from the word box. Then listen. Track 20

Go to the market.

Buy some ___________ ,

1 ___________ , 2 ___________ ,

and 3 ___________ .

Go to the pet shop.

See a ___________ ,

a ___________ , a ___________ ,

and some ___________ . I like fish.

Word Box   cake bananas fish duck dog cookies frog cups

21

Let's Play

Move Move

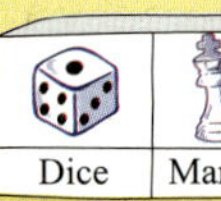

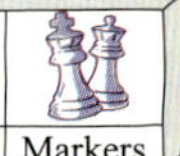

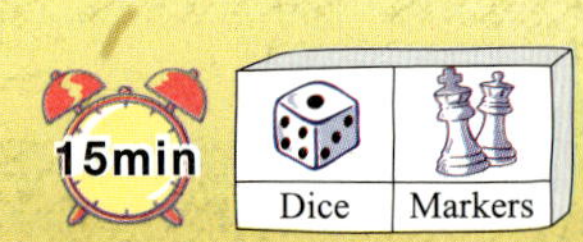

How to play

게임의 규칙은 윷놀이 게임과 동일합니다.

❶ 게임 판 안쪽 돌 안에는 학생들이 어려워하는 알파벳이나 단어 혹은 모음을 써 넣습니다.

❷ 말이 위치한 곳의 알파벳과 소리 또는 단어를 읽고 첫소리를 말하게 하며 먼저 도착한 사람이 승리합니다. 활동 시간이 부족하면 바깥쪽만 게임 판으로 이용해도 됩니다.

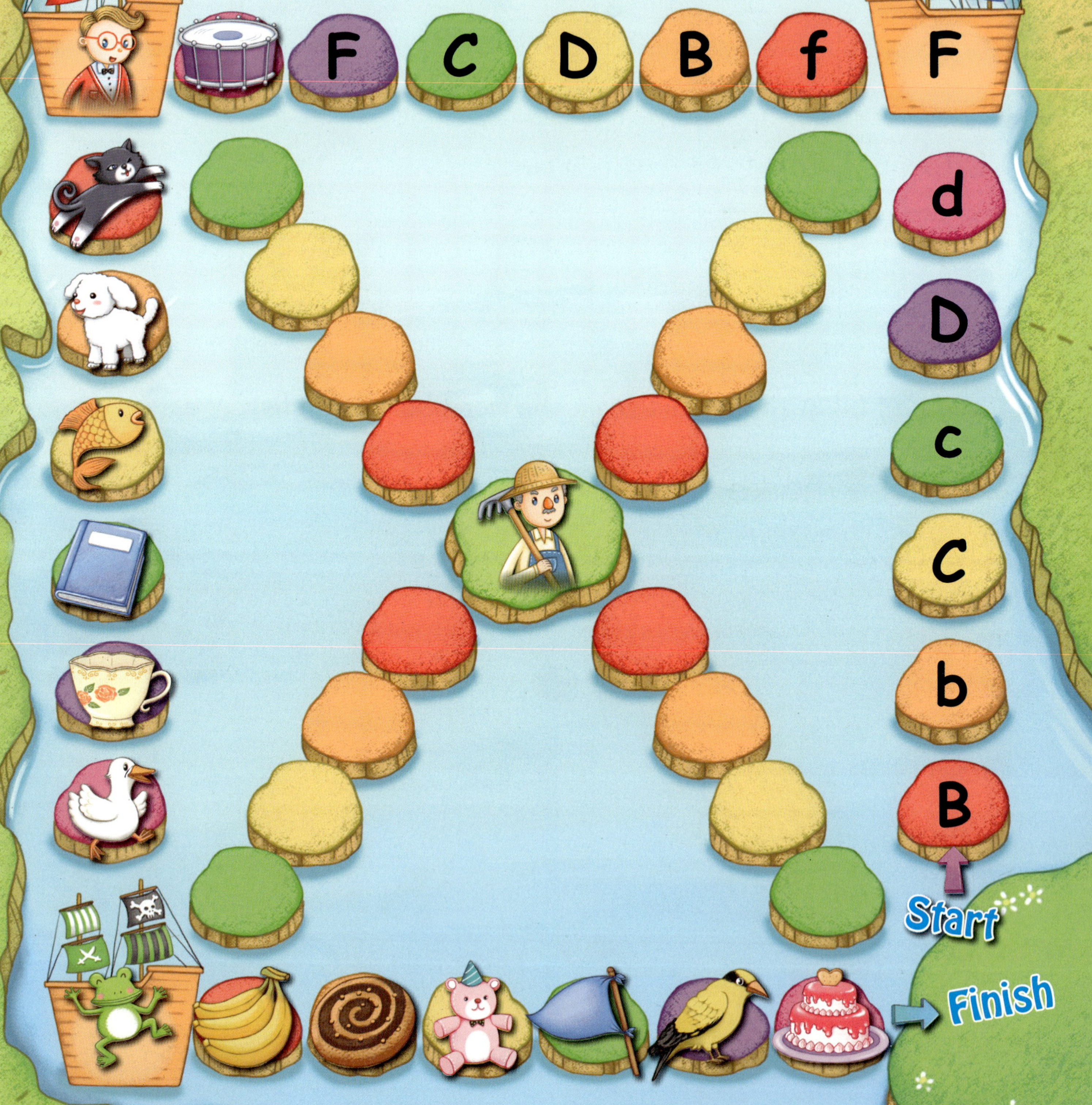

Homework Spot

Track 21

1 Listen and color the correct letter.

① B d **②** c f **③** b d **④** c f

2 Listen and circle the correct picture. Then write the beginning letter.

①   **②**   **③**   **④**  

3 Listen and draw.

4 Listen, read and write the beginning letter.

Go to the pet shop.

See a ____ird ____ , a ____at ____ ,

a ____og ____ , and a ____rog ____ . I like fish.

The Letters and Sounds Gg, Hh, Jj, Kk

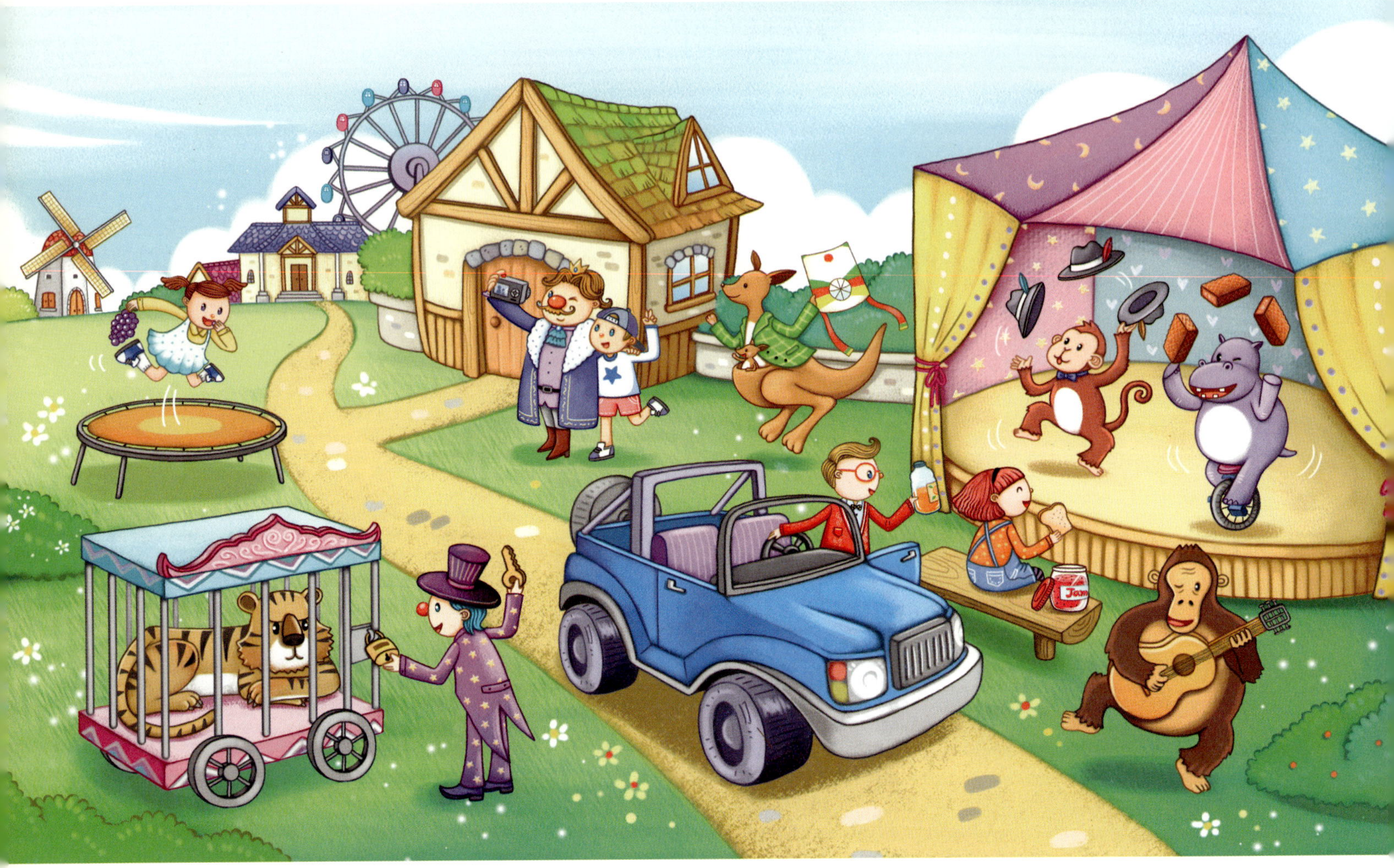

Look and find the new word, then circle.

Listen, repeat and check. Track 22

girl	☐	jam	☐	
gorilla	☐	juice	☐	
guitar	☐	jacket	☐	
grapes	☐	jeep	☐	
ham	☐	king	☐	
hat	☐	key	☐	
hippo	☐	kangaroo	☐	
house	☐	kite	☐	

My Dictionary

Read and write.

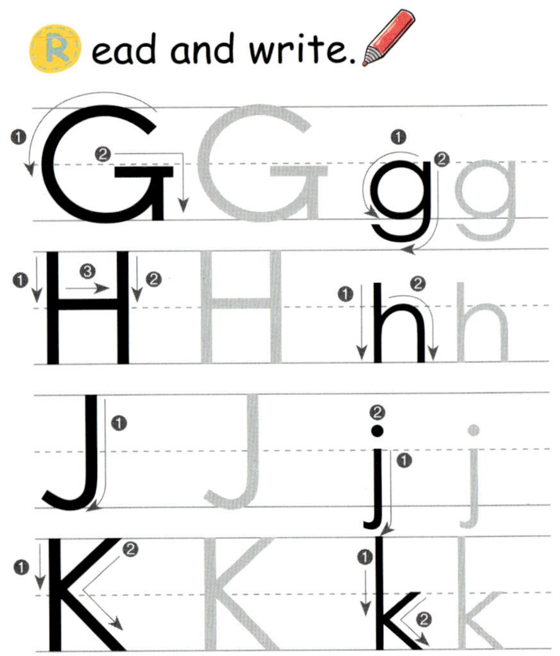

10min

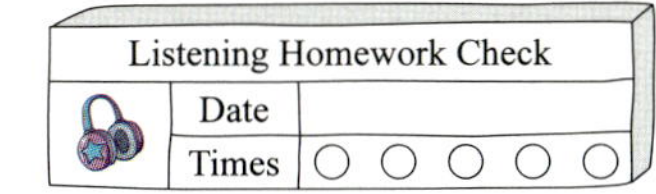

Gg
Hh
Jj
Kk

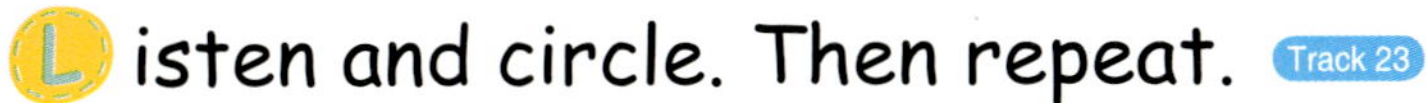

Listen and circle. Then repeat. Track 23

G - g - g says /g/ /g/ .

G - g - g says /g/ /g/ .

H - h - h says /h/ /h/ .

H - h - h says /h/ /h/ .

The girl dances with a gorilla.

The hippo in a hat.

J - j - j says /j/ /j/ .

J - j - j says /j/ /j/ .

K - k - k says /k/ /k/ .

K - k - k says /k/ /k/ .

Pack jam and juice. The kangaroo flies a kite.

POP Quiz   Write the beginning letter.

Score
8

1. ________

2. ________

3. ________

4. ________

5. ________

6. ________

7. ________

8. ________

isten and number. Track 24

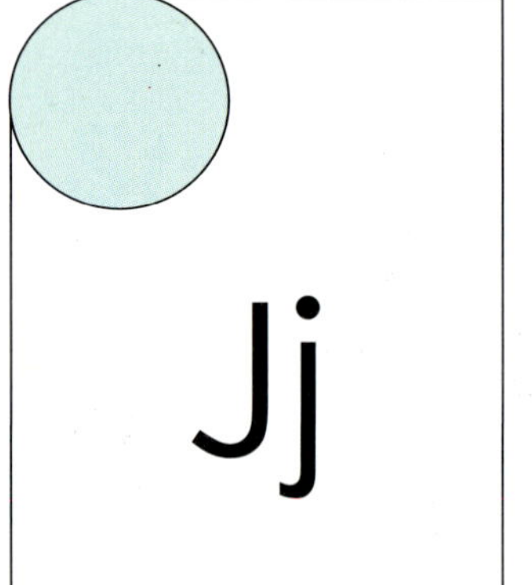
Jj

Kk

Hh

Gg

isten and circle the correct beginning letter. Track 25

1. Gh   Hh

2. Kk   Jj

3. Kk   Jj

4. Gh   Hh

Mini Test Listen and write. Track 26

Score / 5

1. _______ 2. _______ 3. _______ 4. _______ 5. _______

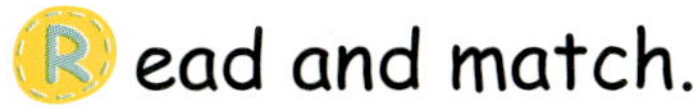

5min

Read and match.

Gg Jj Kk Hh

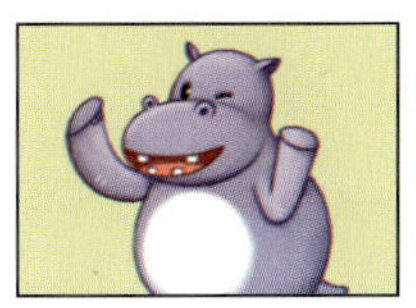

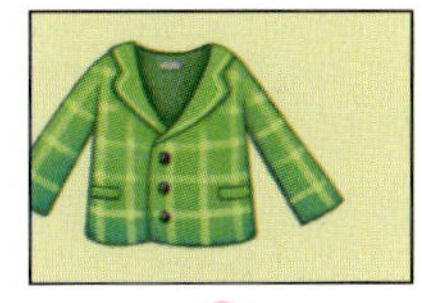

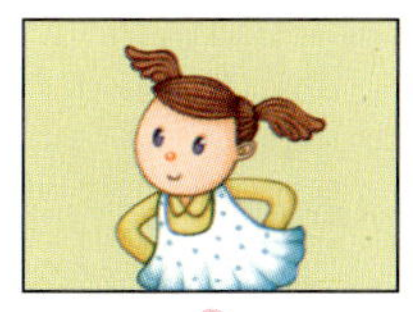

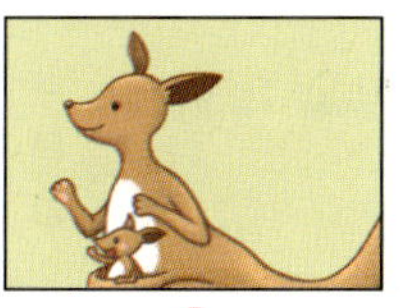

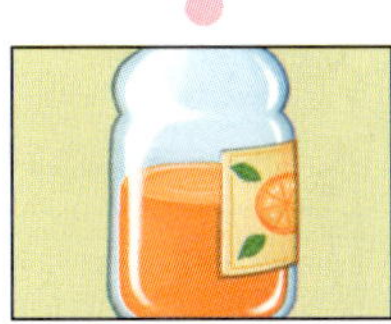

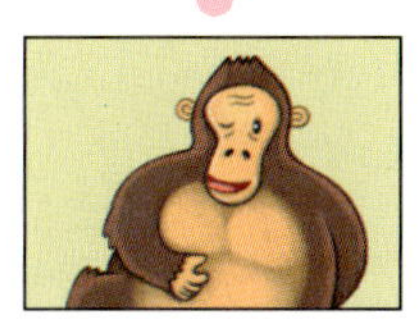

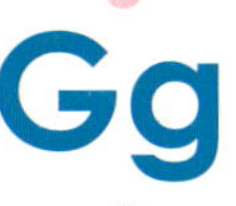

Read and fill in the blanks from the word box.

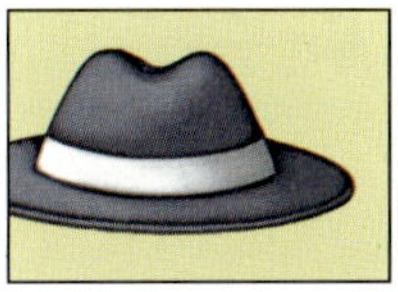

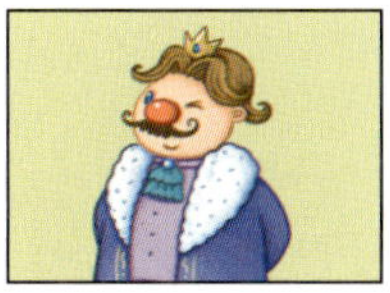

1. See a .
2. Play the .
3. Fly a .
4. Make .

5. Ride a .
6. Try this 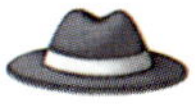 .
7. Jump with a .

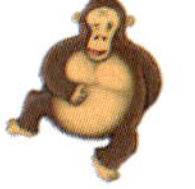

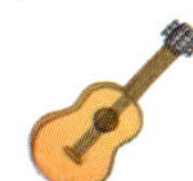

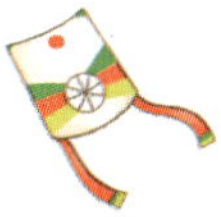

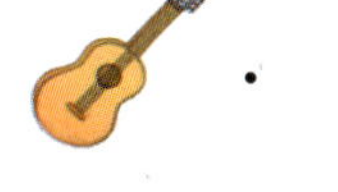

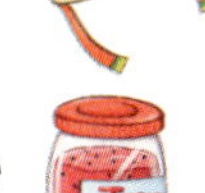

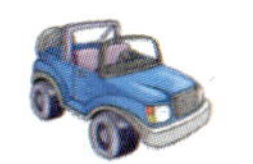

Word Box: jeep kangaroo guitar jam hat gorilla kite

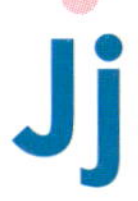

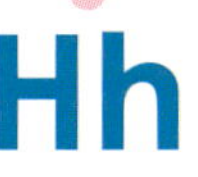

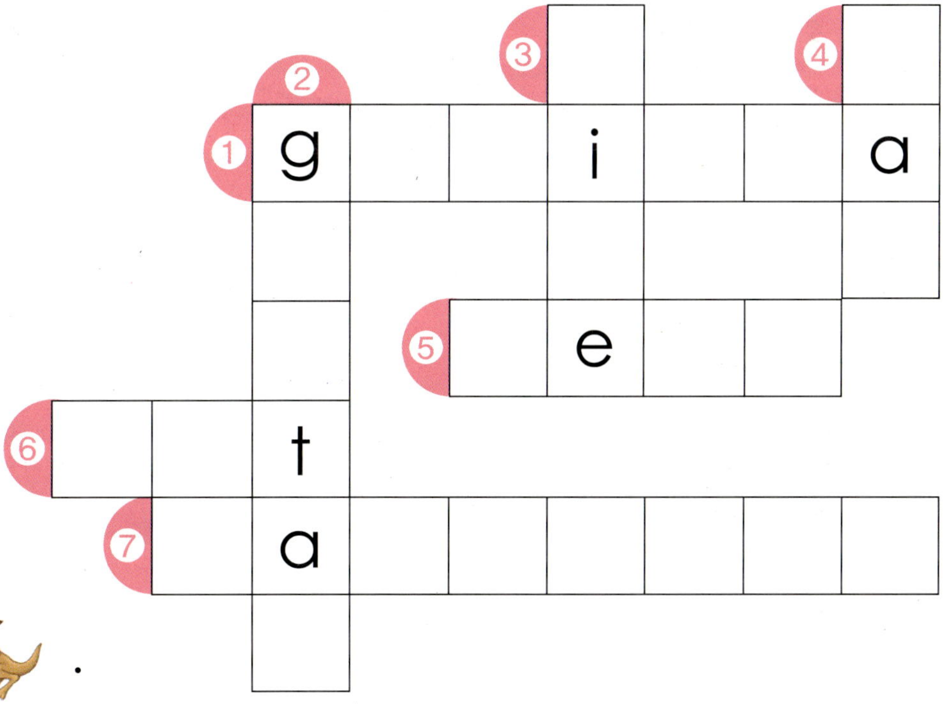

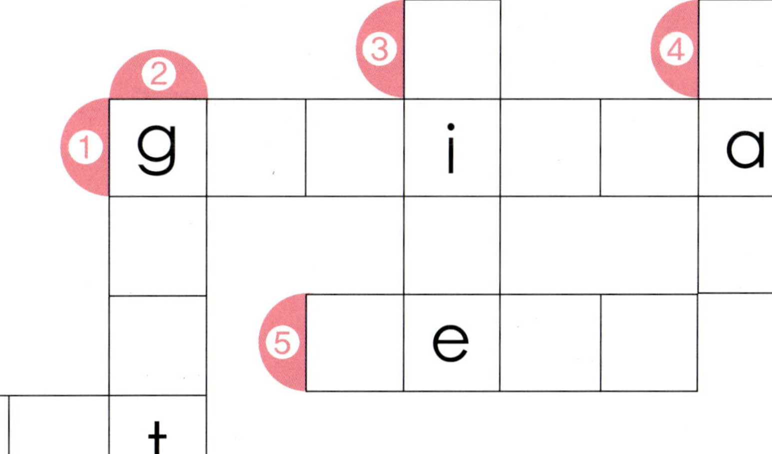

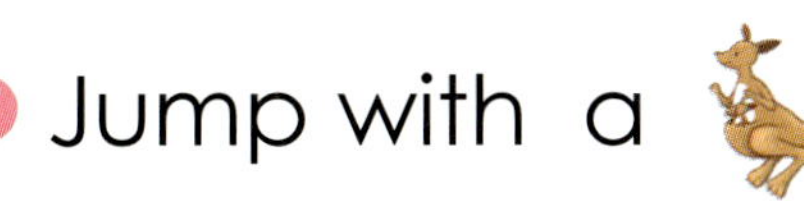

Let's Play
Flick Flick
15min
Coins
Colored pencils
How to play
❶ 각 칸에 Gg, Hh, Jj, Kk를 대소문자로 나눠서 적거나 알파벳 1-3과 복습용 게임 판으로 활용해도 됩니다.
❷ 자신의 start 자리를 정하고 순서를 정한 뒤 자신의 땅을 표시할 색깔을 정합니다.
❸ 동전을 Start 자리에 놓고 튕겨서 위치하는 곳의 알파벳을 읽고 첫소리를 말하면 자기 색깔로 칠할 수 있습니다.(폭탄이 있는 곳은 땅을 차지할 수 없고 이미 다른 사람이 차지한 땅도 자신의 땅으로 색칠할 수 없습니다.)
❹ 모든 땅의 색이 칠해지면 칸의 개수가 많은 사람이 승리하게 됩니다.
Start
Start
Start
Start

Homework Spot `Track 27`

1 Listen and choose check(✔) or cross(✘).

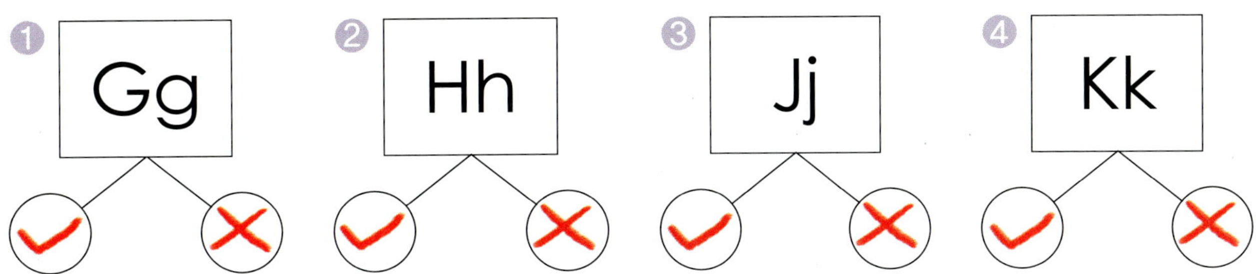

2 Listen and circle. Write.

① girl
house
juice
____

② kite
hippo
jeep
____

③ king
gorilla
ham
____

④ hat
kangaroo
guitar
____

3 Listen and choose the correct picture.

①  

②  

4 Listen, read and write the word from the word box.

See a 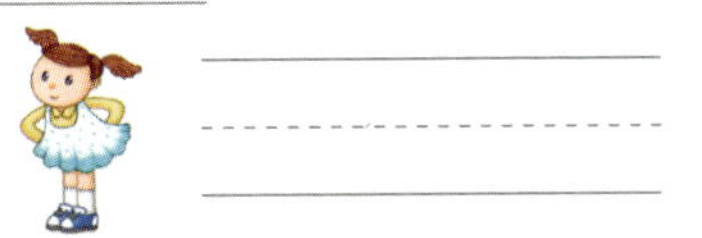 _______________ .   Make a 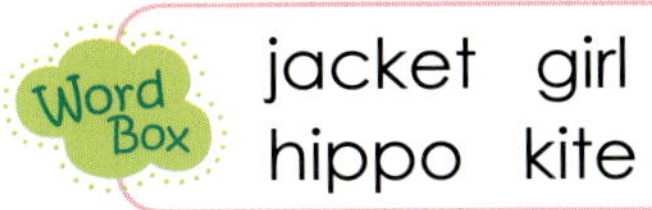 _______________ .

Try this 🧥 _______________ .

Jump up with the 👧 _______________ .

Word Box: jacket girl hippo kite

The Letters and Sounds Ll, Mm, Nn, Pp 

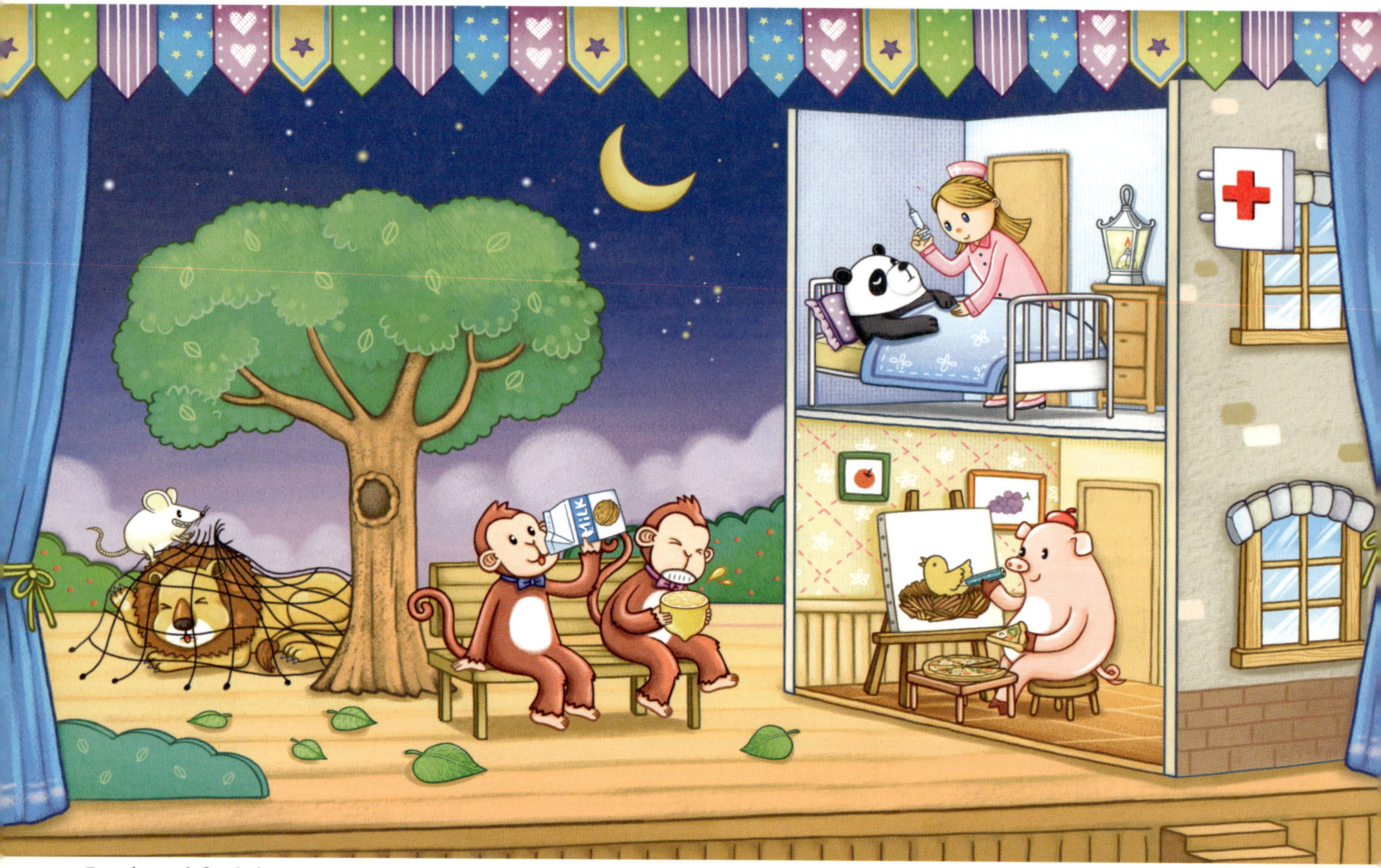

Look and find the new word, then circle.

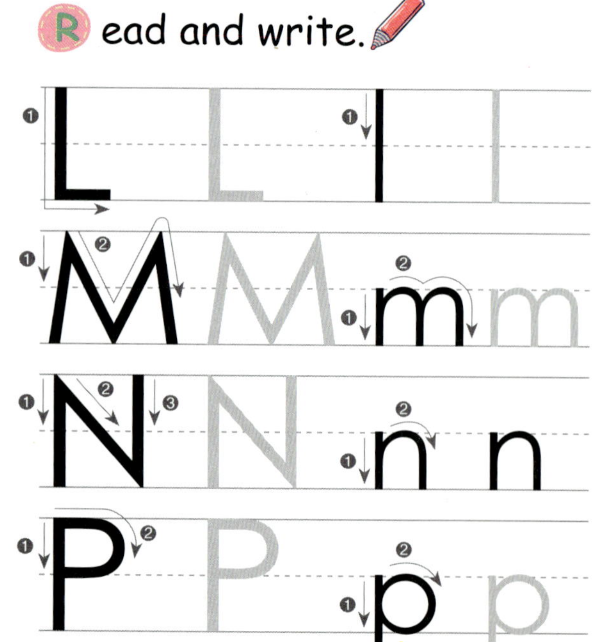

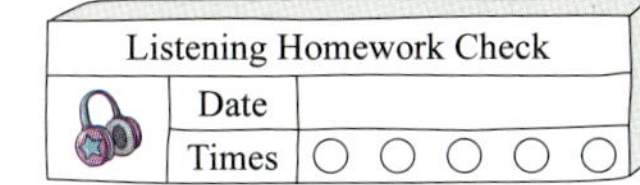

Listen and repeat. Track 29

L - l - l says /l/ /l/  lemon.
L - l - l says /l/ /l/  leaf.
M - m - m says /m/ /m/  mouse.
M - m - m says /m/ /m/  monkey.

The lemon on the leaf. The mouse after a monkey.

N - n - n says /n/ /n/  nut.
N - n - n says /n/ /n/  nest.
P - p - p says /p/ /p/  pig.
P - p - p says /p/ /p/  pencil.

The nut in the nest. The pig with a pencil.

POP QUIZ   Write the beginning letter.

Score
8

1. _______
2. _______
3. _______
4. _______
5. _______
6. _______
7. _______
8. _______

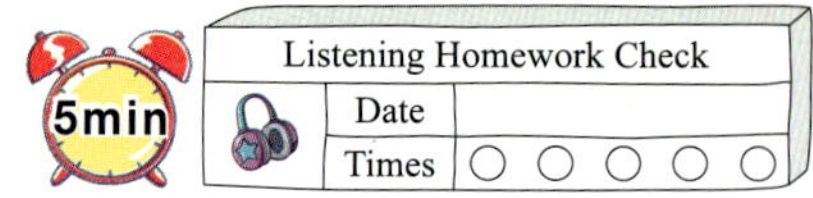

Listen to the word and circle the correct beginning letter. Track 30

1. l m n p

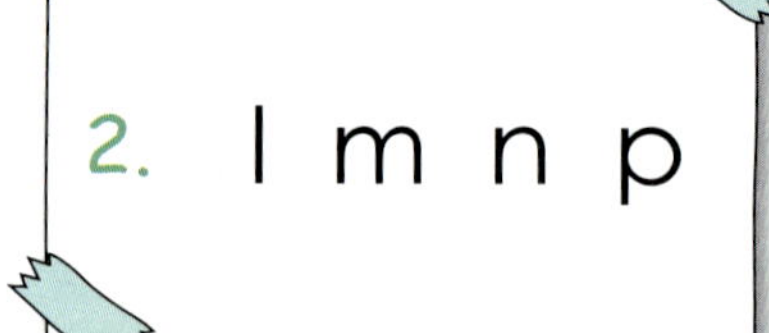
2. l m n p

3. l m n p

4. l m n p

5. l m n p

6. l m n p

Listen to the word and circle the correct picture. Track 31

1.    

2.  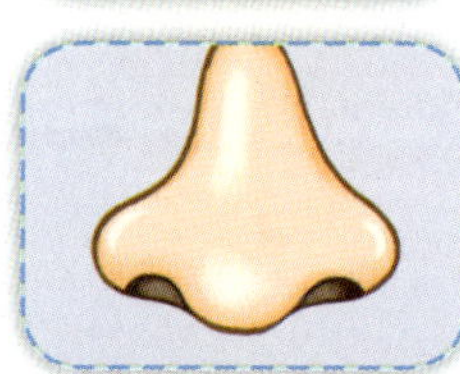  

3.    

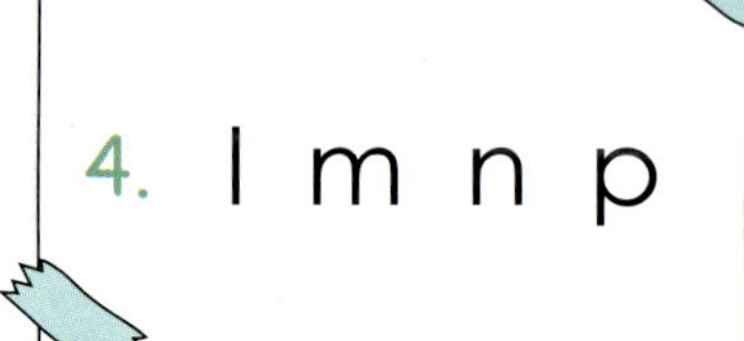

Mini Test Listen and write. Track 32

Score
5

1. _______ 2. _______ 3. _______ 4. _______ 5. _______

L ook and circle the correct word.

Ll
Mm
Nn
Pp

R ead, draw and trace.

Draw a △ on the pizza and panda .

Draw a ☆ on the lemon and leaf .

Draw a ♡ on the mouse and the monkey .

Draw a ◯ on the nurse and nest .

Let's Play
Finding Mom
15min
Dice
Markers
Finish
I m p n m n l p
Start
N L M P N M L P
How to play
❶ 글자에서는 첫소리를, 그림에서는 단어와 첫소리를 말하며 전진해 가장 먼저 도착한 사람이 승리합니다.
❷ 게임은 수업시간을 고려해 1회 또는 2회를 합니다. 가정에서도 게임숙제를 하고 그 결과에 따라 얼굴을 색칠하게 합니다.
1st round
2nd round
In the class
At home

Homework Spot　Track 33

1 Listen and choose the correct letter.

① l　m　n　p　　　② l　m　n　p　　　③ l　m　n　p

④ l　m　n　p　　　⑤ l　m　n　p　　　⑥ l　m　n　p

2 Listen and write the letter in order.

① ⟶ ② ⟶ ③ ⟶ ④

3 Listen and circle the picture.

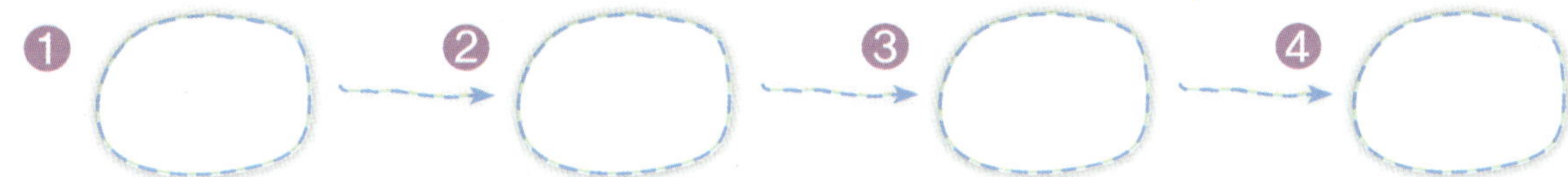

L - l - l says /l/ /l/  . The lemon on the leaf.

M - m - m says /m/ /m/  .
The mouse after a monkey .

N - n - n says /n/ /n/  . The nut in the nest.

P - p - p says /p/ /p/  . The pig with a pencil.

4 Look, listen and circle.

Unit 06

The Letters and Sounds Qq, Rr, Ss, Tt

Look and find the new word, then circle.

Listen, repeat and check. Track 34

queen ☐
question ☐
quilt ☐
quarter ☐
rabbit ☐
robot ☐
ring ☐
ribbon ☐

sun ☐
six ☐
spider ☐
sofa ☐
tiger ☐
tomato ☐
truck ☐
table ☐

My Dictionary

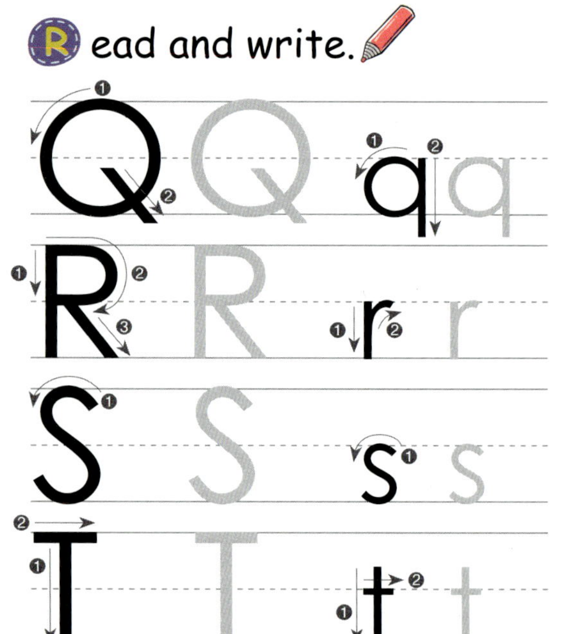

 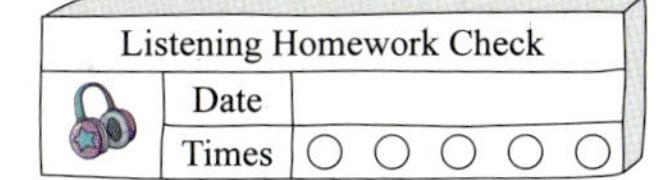

Unit 06

Qq
Rr
Ss
Tt

Listen and repeat, then trace. Track 35

Q - q - q says /q/ /q/ queen .
Q - q - q says /q/ /q/ question .
R - r - r says /r/ /r/ rabbit .
R - r - r says /r/ /r/ ring .

The queen has a question. The rabbit has a ring.

S - s - s says /s/ /s/ six .
S - s - s says /s/ /s/ spider .
T - t - t says /t/ /t/ tomato .
T - t - t says /t/ /t/ truck .

Six spiders on the web. Tomatoes on the truck.

Write the beginning letter.

Score
8

1.   2.   3.   4.

5.   6.   7.   8.

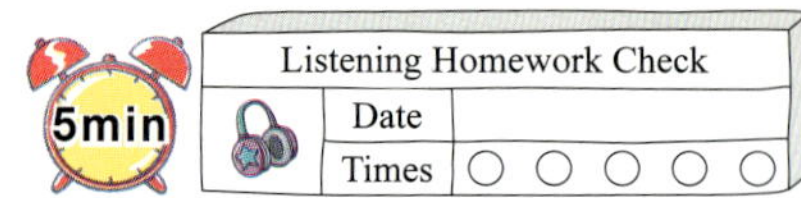

Listen and circle "Yes" if both have the same beginning sound, or "No" if not. Track 36

1.  Yes — No

2.  Yes — No

3. 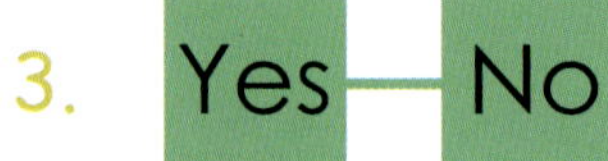 Yes — No

4. Yes — No

5. Yes — No

6. Yes — No

Listen and match the balloon to the picture and the correct letter. Track 37

 1  2  3  4  5  6

Mini Test Listen and write. Track 38

Score
5

1. ____   2. ____   3. ____   4. ____   5. ____

Fill in the circle next to the correct beginning letter sound for each picture. (5min)

Qq Rr Ss Tt

1. 
   q ○
   r ○
   s ○

2. 
   q ○
   r ○
   s ○

3.
   r ○
   s ○
   t ○

4. 
   r ○
   s ○
   t ○

5. 
   s ○
   t ○
   q ○

6. 
   s ○
   t ○
   q ○

7. 
   t ○
   q ○
   r ○

8. 
   t ○
   q ○
   r ○

9.
   r ○
   q ○
   t ○

Look and fill in the blanks from the word box. Then listen. Track 39

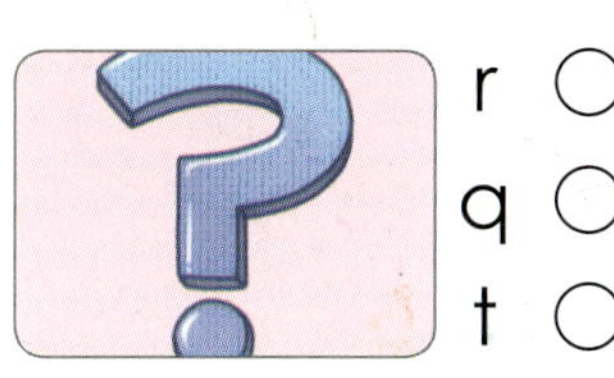

The _____________ is on the _____________ .
The _____________ is at the _____________ .

Fold the _____________ into _____________ .
The _____________ has a _____________ .

Word Box: ring   queen   quilt   tiger   robot   quarter   sofa   table

❶ Tic-Tac-Toe 게임을 하기 전에 각 그림 아래 동그라미에 첫소리 글자를 모두 적으며 복습합니다.
❷ O, X 카드를 오려 Tic-Tac-Toe 칸 위에 글자의 소리 또는 첫소리 글자를 말하며 놓습니다.
❸ 먼저 대각선이나 가로 혹은 세로줄을 먼저 만든 사람이 이깁니다.
❹ Game 1은 알파벳을 말하고 첫소리를 내야 하며 Game 2는 단어를 읽고 첫소리 글자를 말한다. Game 3은 자율적으로 칸을 채운 뒤 게임합니다.

40

 Homework Spot 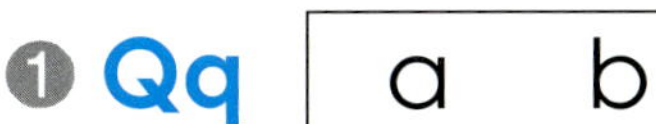 Track 40

Qq Rr Ss Tt

1 Listen to the each word and circle the same beginning sound.

❶ **Qq**   a   b   c   ❷ **Rr**   a   b   c

❸ **Ss**   a   b   c   ❹ **Tt**   a   b   c

2 Listen and write the beginning letter.

❶    ❷    ❸    ❹    ❺ 

____________ ____________ ____________ ____________ ____________

3 Listen and circle the correct word.

The [queen / robot] has a question. The rabbit has a [tiger / ring] .

[Six / Ten] spiders on the web. Tomatoes on the [sofa / truck] .

4 Look, listen and circle.

The Letters and Sounds Vv, Ww, Xx, Yy, Zz

Look and find the new word, then circle.

Listen, repeat and check. Track 41

- violin ☐
- vest ☐
- vase ☐
- van ☐
- watch ☐
- walk ☐
- water ☐
- web ☐
- xylophone ☐
- X-ray ☐
- yo-yo ☐
- yogurt ☐
- yell ☐
- zoo ☐
- zero ☐
- zebra ☐

My Dictionary

Read and write.

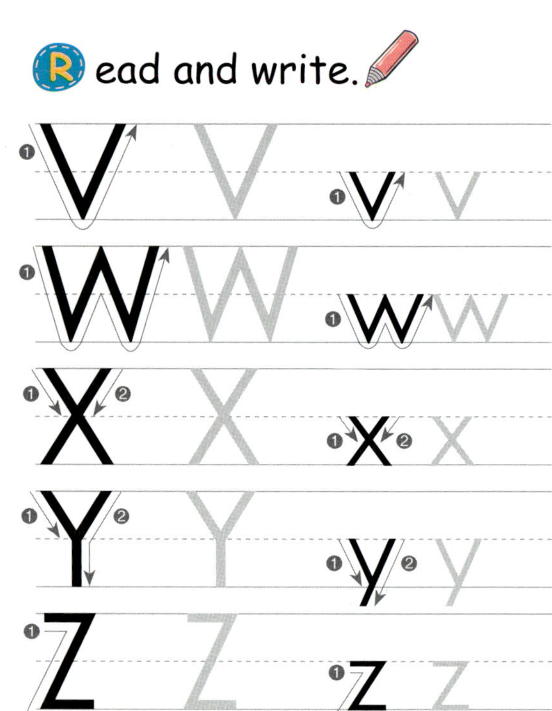

Let's Chant 10min

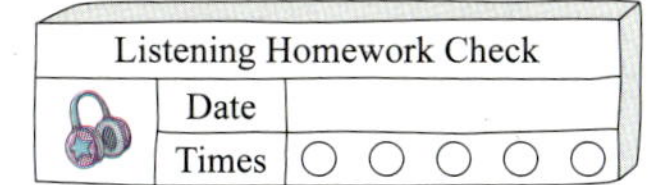

Vv
Ww
Xx
Yy
Zz

Listen and circle. Then repeat. Track 42

V - v - v says /v/ /v/ 　　 .
V - v - v says /v/ /v/ 　　 .
W - w - w says /w/ /w/ 　　 .
W - w - w says /w/ /w/ 　　 .

The violin is by the vase. Walk in the water.

X - x - x says /x/ /x/ 　　 .
Y - y - y says /y/ /y/ 　　 .
Z - z - z says /z/ /z/ 　　 .

We play the xylophone and
yo-yo at the zoo.

POP QUIZ Write the beginning letter.

Score
8

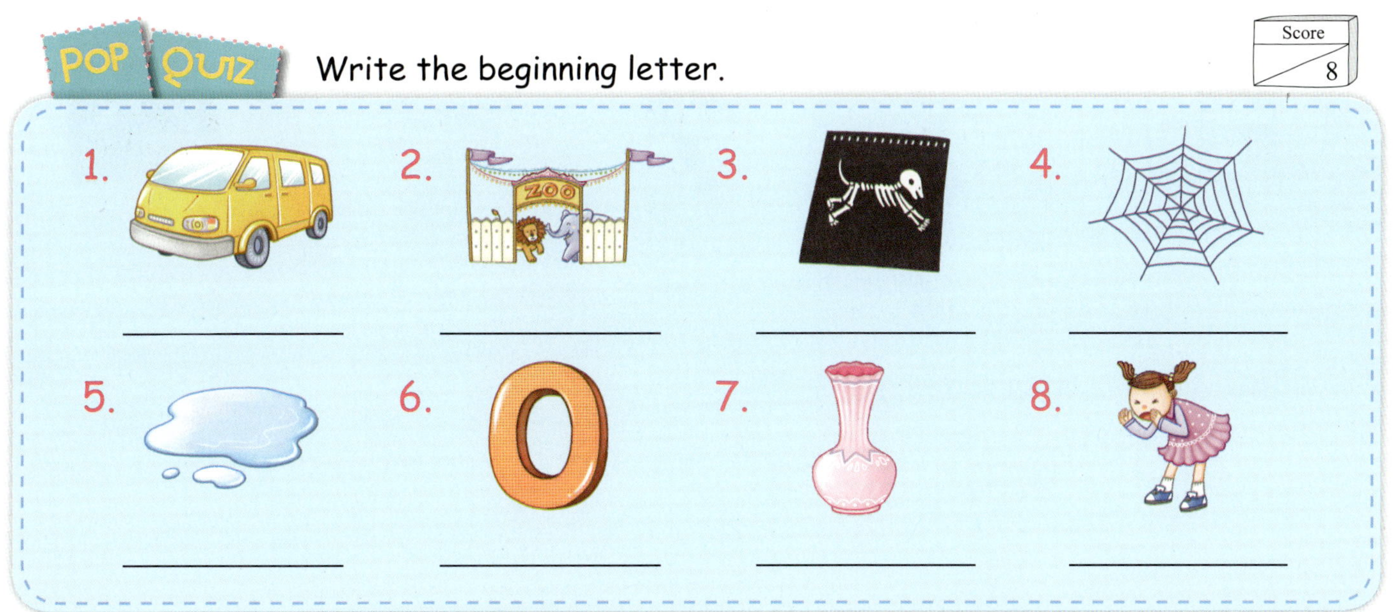

Listen to the sound and circle the right picture. Track 43 5min

1.
2.
3.
4.
5.
6.

Listen and write the missing letter. Draw a line to the picture. Track 44

1. ☐ -ray 2. ☐ oo 3. ☐ ogurt 4. ☐ alk 5. ☐ ase

Mini Test Listen and write. Track 45

Score
5

1. _______ 2. _______ 3. _______ 4. _______ 5. _______

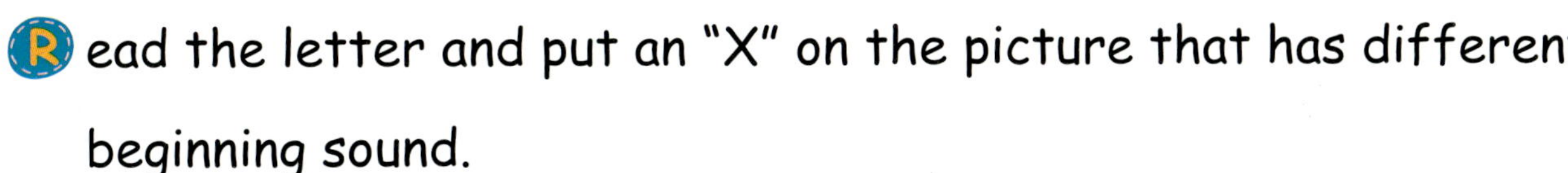

®ead the letter and put an "X" on the picture that has different beginning sound.

Vv			
Ww			
Xx			
Yy			
Zz			

Vv Ww Xx Yy Zz

®ead and fill in the blanks from the word box. Then listen. Track 46

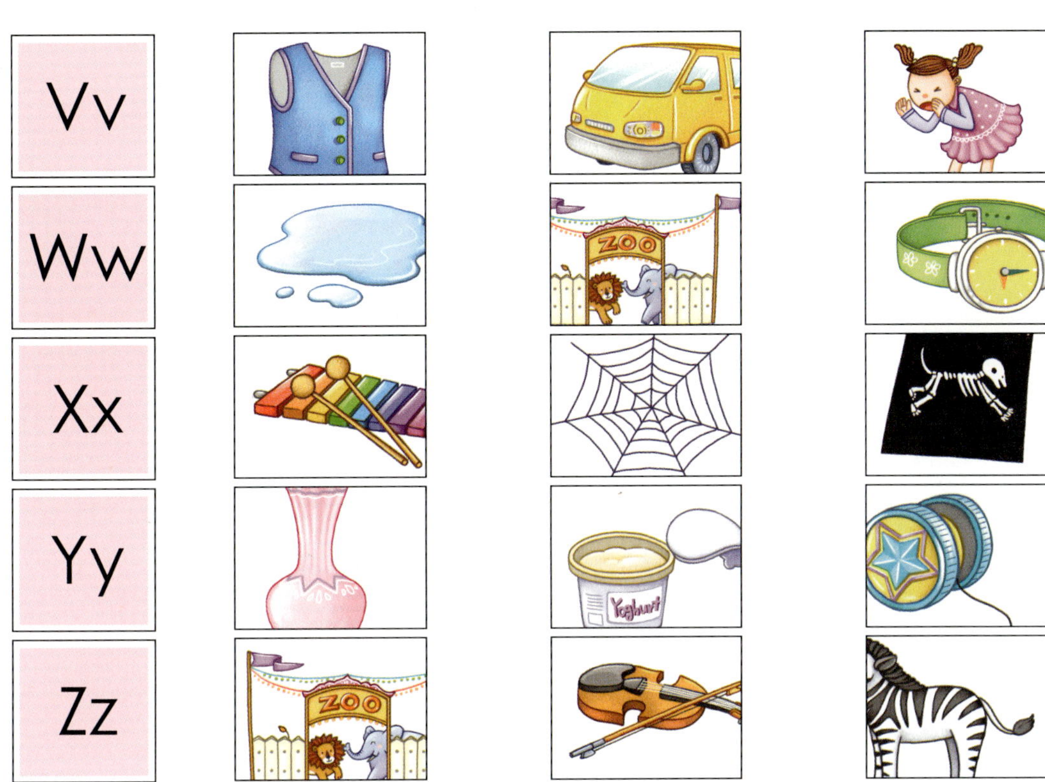

Put on a ___________ .

and a ___________ .

Don't ___________ .

Here is ___________ .

Go to the ___________ .

Look at the ___________ .

It looks sick. Take an ___________ .

Word Box   vest yogurt zoo yell watch zebra X-ray

45

How to play

❶ 게임 판의 빈칸에는 학생들이 어려워하는 알파벳이나 단어를 써 넣습니다.

❷ 주사위를 던져 말이 위치한 곳의 알파벳과 소리 또는 단어를 읽고 첫소리를 말하며 전진해 먼저 도착한 사람이 승리합니다.

1 Listen and circle the correct letter.

2 Listen and circle the correct picture. Then write the beginning letter.

3 Listen and circle.

4 Listen, read and write the word.

Go to the  _________ .   Look at the _________ .

It looks sick.   Take an  _________ .

The Short "a" Sound

Look and find the new word, then circle.

Listen, repeat and check. Track 48

- cat ☐
- hat ☐
- fat ☐
- bat ☐
- mat ☐
- sad ☐
- dad ☐

- ham ☐
- ram ☐
- jam ☐
- fan ☐
- can ☐
- cap ☐
- map ☐

My Dictionary

Listen and write. Track 49

1. f _____ t
2. v _____ n
3. h _____ m
4. c _____ p

Let's Chant  10min

Listen and repeat. Track 50

Fat cat, fat cat,
A fat cat on the ram.

Ham, jam, ham, jam,
ham and jam on the ram.

Can, fan, can, fan
A can and a fan on the mat.

Cap, map, cap, map
A cap and a map on the mat.

POP QUIZ Fill in the blanks.

1. ___ at
2. ___ a ___
3. s ___ ___ ___
4. h ___ ___
5. j ___ ___
6. ___ ___ at
7. ___ a ___
8. ___ a ___

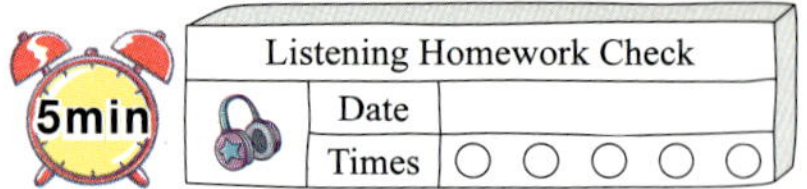

Listen and circle the correct word. `Track 51` 5min

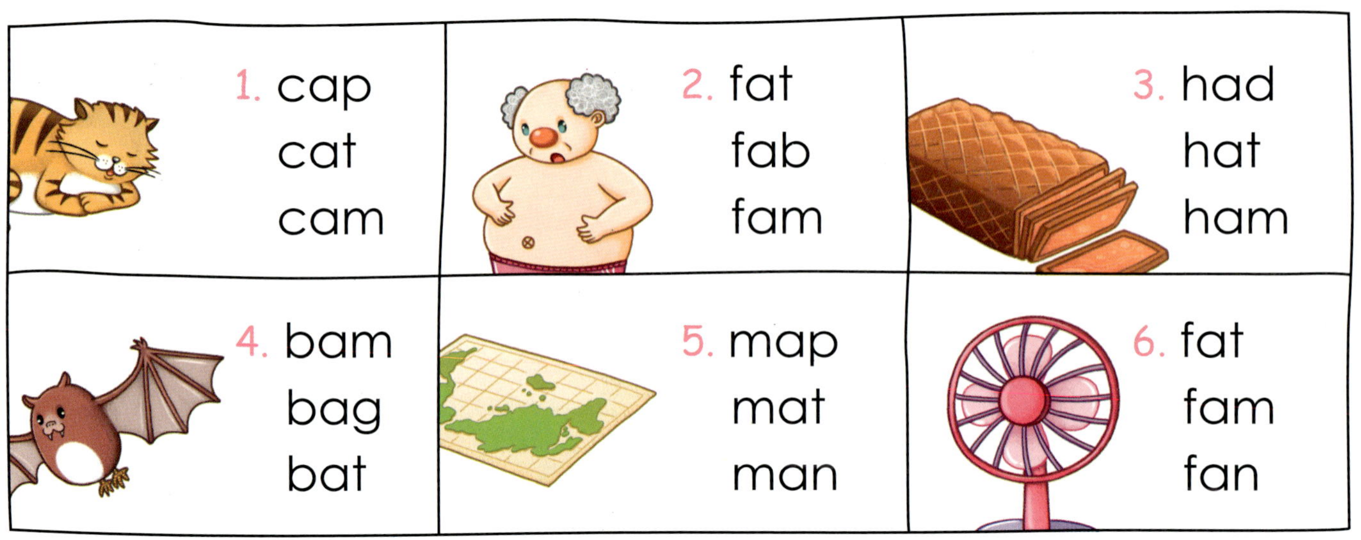

Listen and number, then read. `Track 52`

Mini Test Listen and write. `Track 53`

Score
5

1. _______ 2. _______ 3. _______ 4. _______ 5. _______

50

C ircle the correct word and write. Then listen. `Track 54` 5min

This is a _______ cat. **fat** **mat**

The cat is on a _______ . **mat** **ham**

"I have a _______ ." **cap** **can**

This is a _______ . **ram** **bat**

The bat is on a _______ . **hat** **fat**

"I have ham and _______ ." **jam** **fan** "Let's have a party."

C omplete the crossword puzzle.

1. f

2. a

3. m

4. d

5. a

6. p

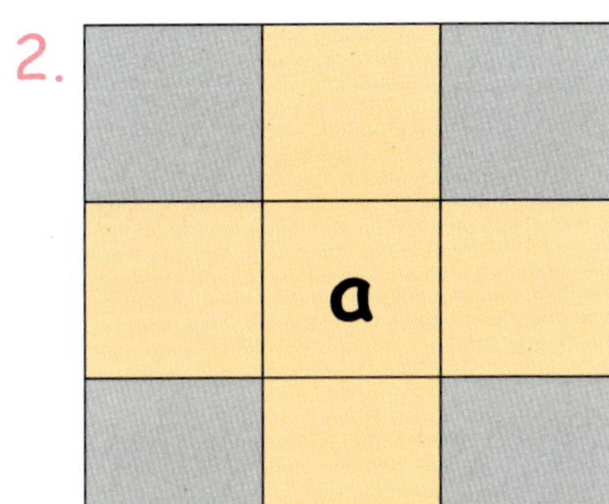

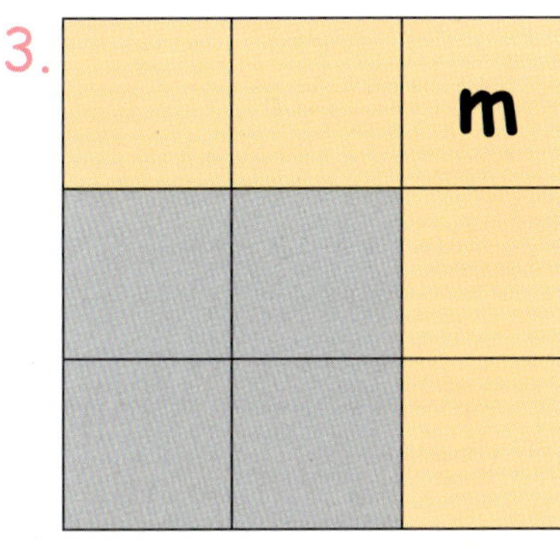

Across

Down

Let's Play

Going to Neverland

15min | Dice | Markers

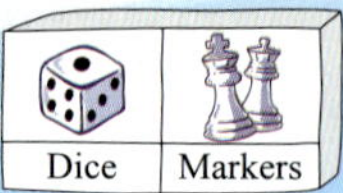

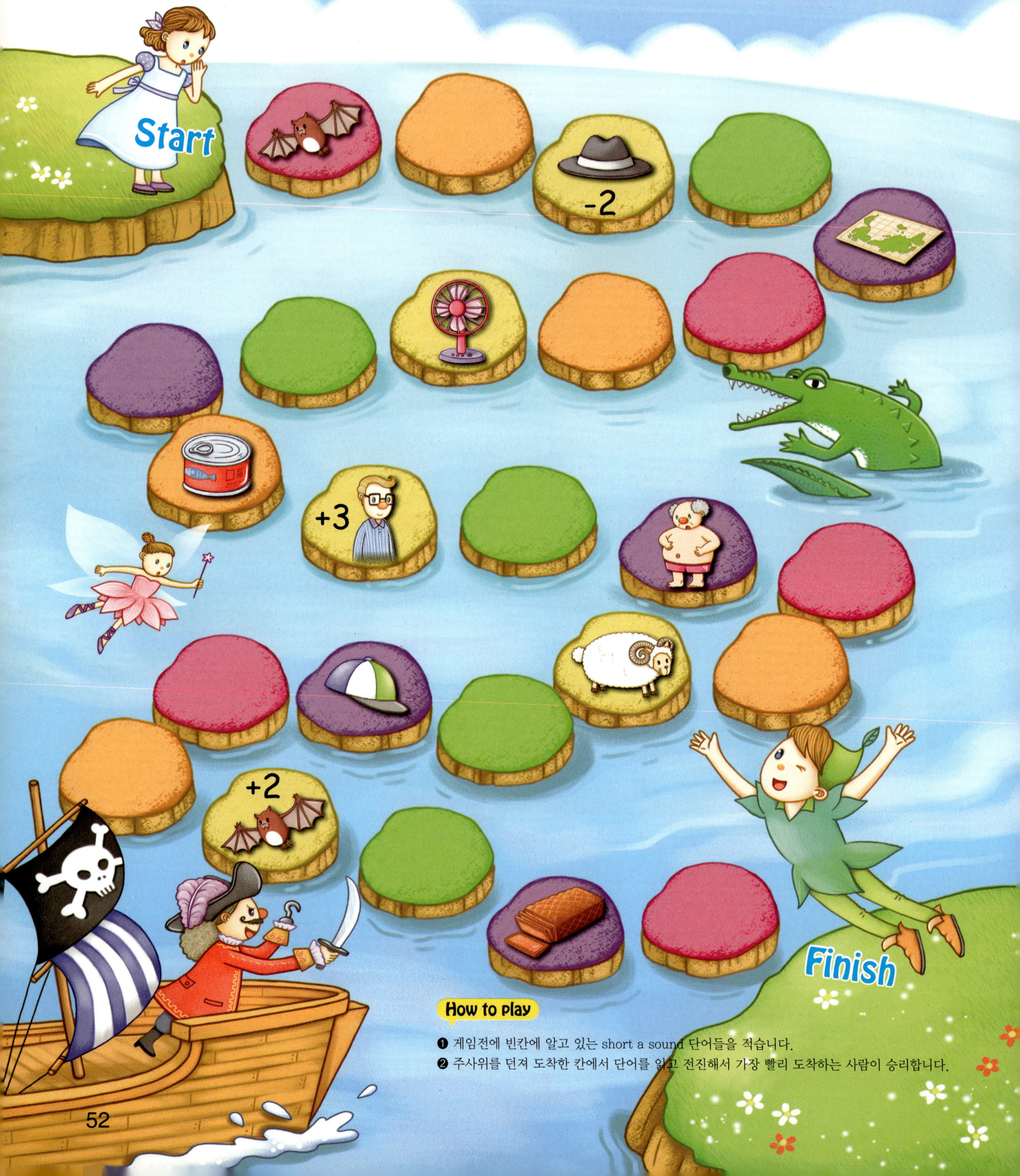

How to play

❶ 게임전에 빈칸에 알고 있는 short a sound 단어들을 적습니다.
❷ 주사위를 던져 도착한 칸에서 단어를 읽고 전진해서 가장 빨리 도착하는 사람이 승리합니다.

Homework Spot `Track 55`

1 Listen and circle a check if they are same rhyming words or a cross if not.

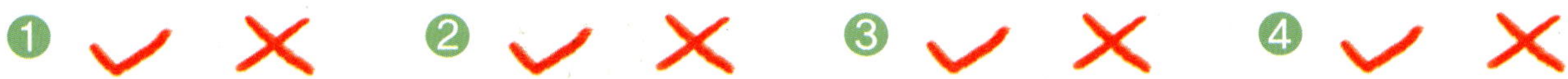

2 Listen and circle. Then write.

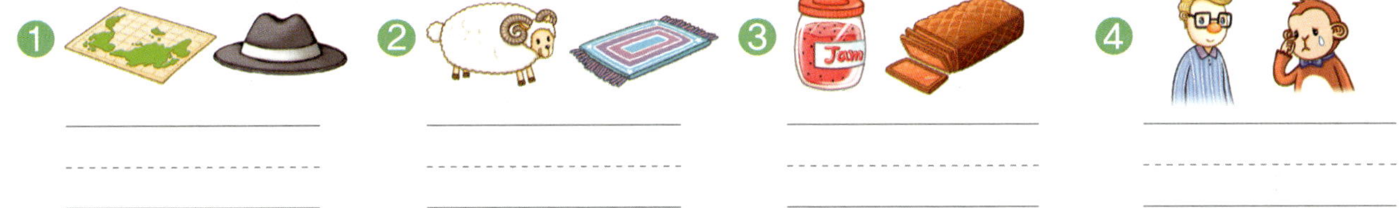

3 Listen and choose the correct letter. Then write.

① n f h a m

② h a m x s

③ a b r t p

4 Read and write the word from the word box, then listen.

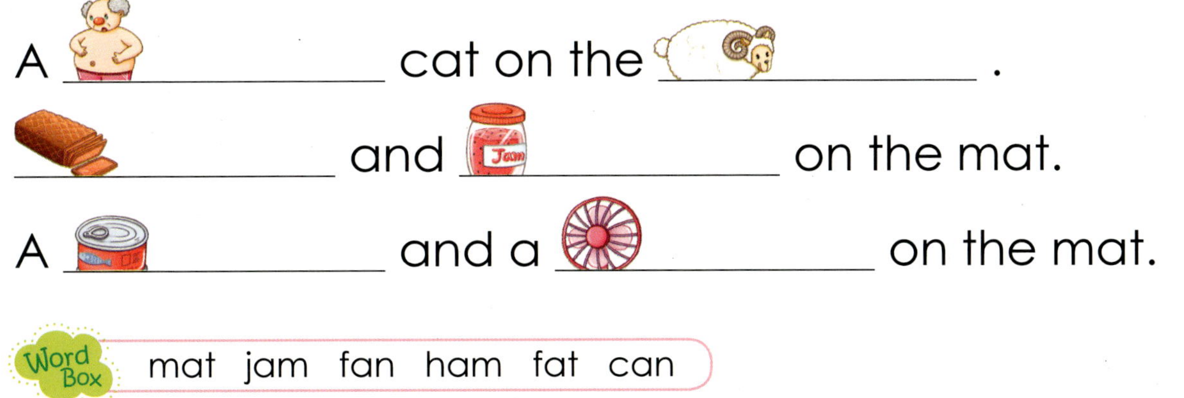

Word Box   mat jam fan ham fat can

The Short "e" Sound

10min

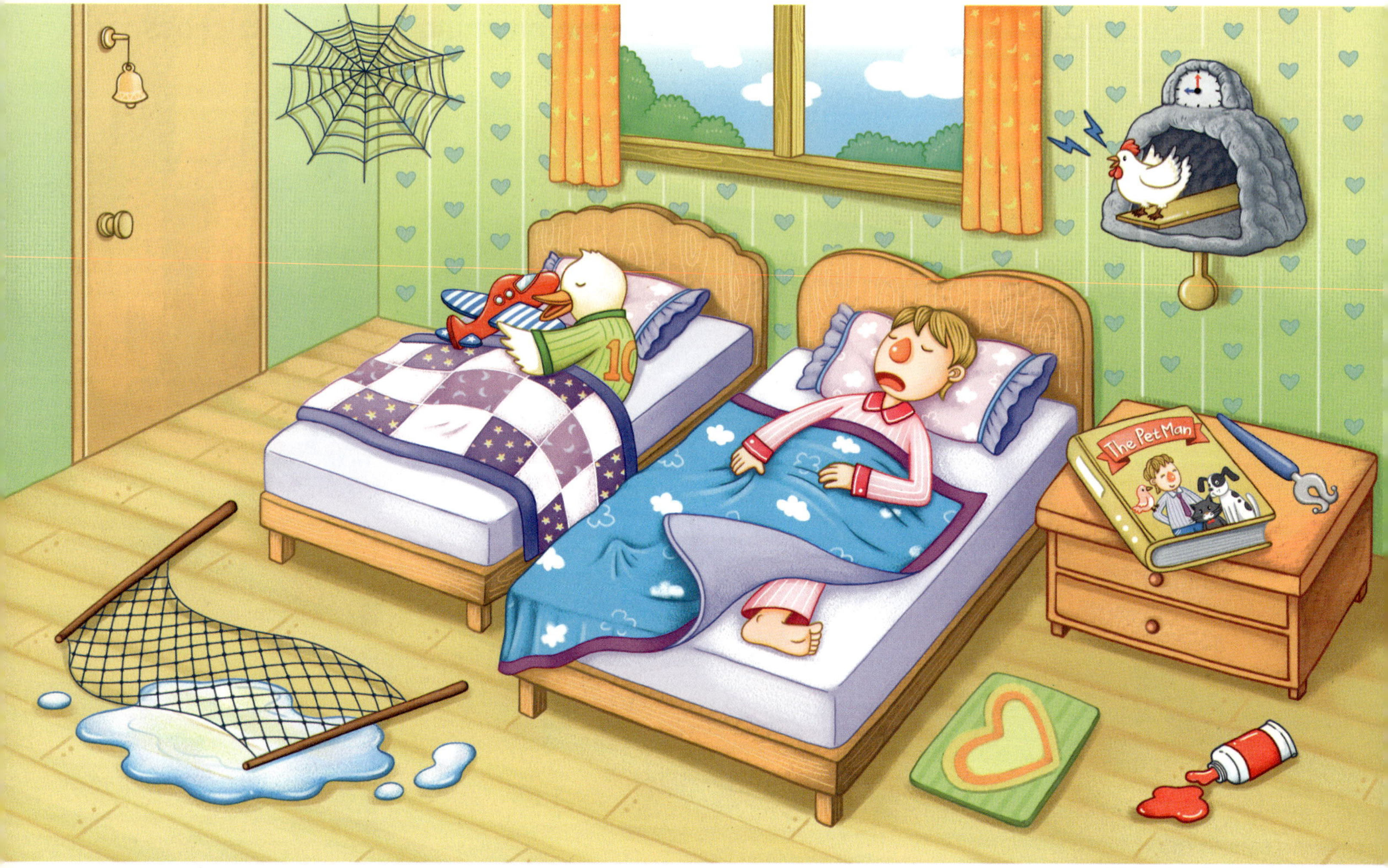

Look and find the new word, then circle.

Listen, repeat and check. Track 56

hen	☐	leg	☐
den	☐	bell	☐
pen	☐	jet	☐
men	☐	wet	☐
ten	☐	net	☐
red	☐	pet	☐
bed	☐	web	☐

My Dictionary

Listen and write. Track 57

1. n ___ t
2. w ___ b
3. m ___ n
4. b ___ ll

Let's Chant  10min

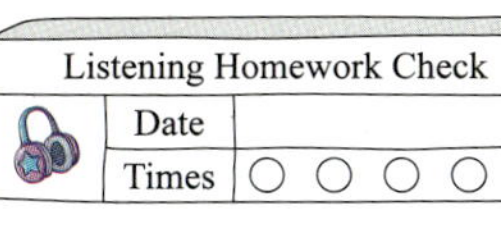

L isten and repeat. Track 58

Ten men, ten men
Ten men are wet.

Red pen, red pen
The red pen is on the bed.

Hen leg, hen leg
The hen has two legs.

Bell, jet, bell, jet
A bell and a jet on the net.

POP QUIZ Fill in the blanks.

Score 8

Listen to the sound and circle the correct picture. Track 59 5min

1.
2.
3.

4.
5.
6.

Listen and write the missing letter. Draw a line to the picture. Track 60

1. □ e □ •   •
2. □ e □ •   •
3. □ e □ •   •
4. □ e □ •   •

Mini Test Listen and write. Track 61

Score
5

1. ________ 2. ________ 3. ________ 4. ________ 5. ________

C ircle the correct word and write, then listen. `Track 62`

In the den,

The red _____ has a net. (hen) (leg)

The _____ is wet. (men) (net)

The hen is not _____ . (web) (wet)

In a jet,

here are ten _____ . (nets) (pens)

Here are six _____ . (bells) (pets)

Ten _____ in a jet. (bed) (men)

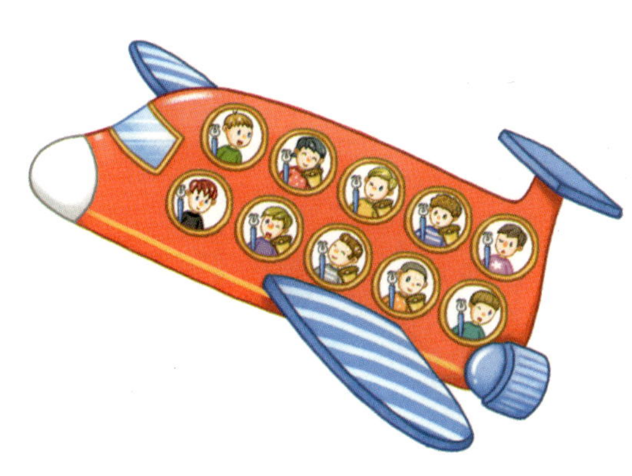

F ind and circle the word.

	j e t s e t d e n l
	r d l e r e d f e n
	p e g f w e t l e g
	p w e t m e s p e g
	d e m b p j e t e r

Search Search Words

How to play

❶ 자신의 땅을 칠할 색을 정한 뒤 가위 바위 보를 합니다.

❷ 제한시간 한번에 약 10초 정도로 한 개의 단어와 그림을 찾으면 동그라미하고, 그림에 체크한 뒤 2점을 줍니다. 단어만 찾은 경우에는 1점을 줍니다.

❸ 제한시간 안에 못 찾으면 순서는 다음 사람에게 넘어가고, 찾은 단어와 그림을 점수로 계산해서 점수가 많은 사람이 승리합니다.

Homework Spot `Track 63`

1 Listen and color the word with the rhyming sound.

❶ 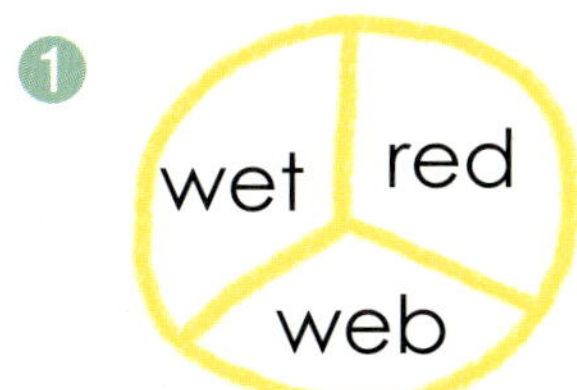

❷ 

❸ 

2 Listen and circle the correct picture. Then write the word.

❶ 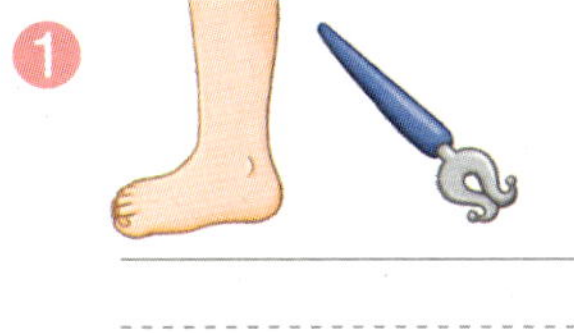

❷ 

❸ 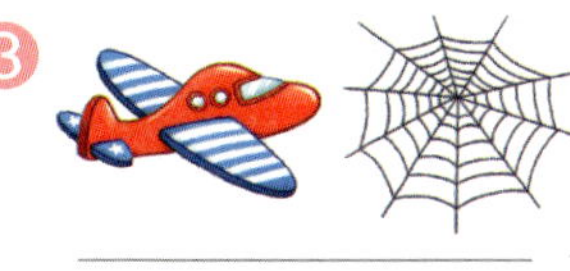

❹ 

3 Listen and match.

❶  ❷  ❸  ❹ 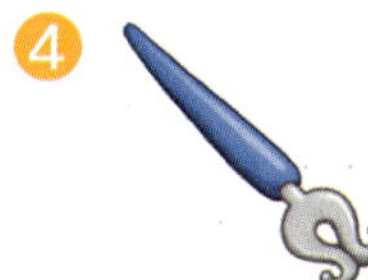 ❺ 

4 Listen and fill in the blanks.

❶ 

Ten _____ are wet.

❷ 

The red _____ is on the bed.

❸ 

The _____ has two legs.

The Short "i" Sound

Look and find the new word, then circle.

Listen, repeat and check. Track 64

- [ ] big
- [ ] wig
- [ ] pig
- [ ] hit
- [ ] sit
- [ ] mitt
- [ ] pin
- [ ] fin
- [ ] win
- [ ] dish
- [ ] fish
- [ ] bib
- [ ] six
- [ ] fix

My Dictionary

Listen and write. Track 65

1. f ___ x
2. w ___ g
3. w ___ n
4. m ___ tt

 **Let's Chant**  10min

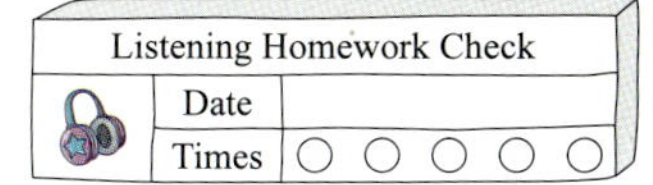

Listen and repeat. Track 66

Big wig, big wig
A big wig on the pig.

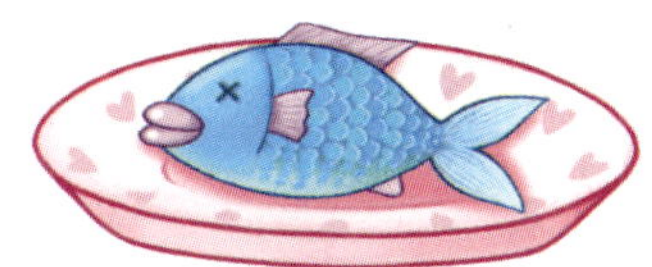

Fish, dish, fish, dish
Fish on the dish.

Six, fix, six, fix
Six pigs fix the car.

Hit, sit, hit, sit
Hit and sit on the bench.

POP QUIZ Fill in the blanks.

Score / 8

1. ___ish

2. ___i___

3. h______

4. ___i___

5. w______

6. ___ib

7. ___i___

8. s______

Listen and circle. Track 67

1. dish
   fin
   big

2. sit
   bib
   fix

3. win
   hit
   pin

4. wig
   fish
   pig

5. mitt
   six
   hit

6. bib
   wig
   six

Listen and circle the picture that has the different rhyme. Track 68

1.   

2.   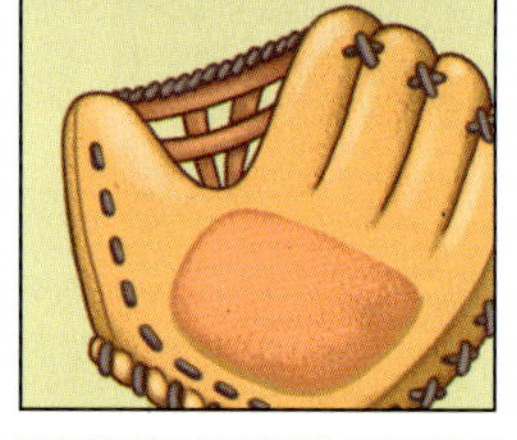

3.   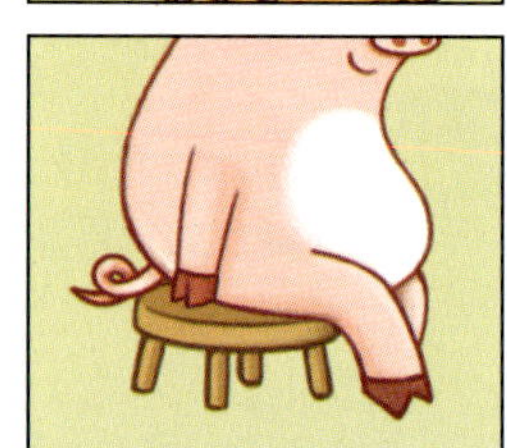

Mini Test - Listen and write. Track 69

1. ____ 2. ____ 3. ____ 4. ____ 5. ____

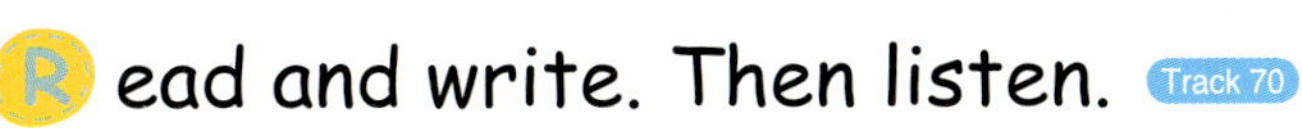 **R**ead and write. Then listen. Track 70 5min

Here are six ________ .   fish   dish

Here is a ________ .   bib   big

Six fish are on the ________ .   dish   pin

This is a big ________ .   big   pig

It has a ________ .   wig   fin

It sits on the ________ .   win   mitt

 **L**ook and circle the correct word.

1.
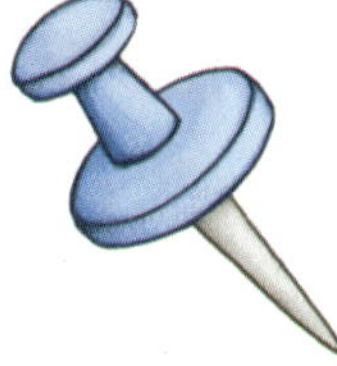
fin   pin

2.

pig   big

3.

fish   dish

4.

hit   sit

5.

wig   mitt

6.

fix   six

Let's Play
Bingo
15min
How to play
❶ Game 1,2 빙고판에 short i 단어를 적고 빙고 게임을 합니다.
❷ One Line Bingo는 단어 10개를 10칸에 순서에 상관없이 적게 한 뒤 순서를 정하고 빙고 칸까지 일직선으로
단어를 지우면서 빙고를 외치면 이기는 게임입니다.
Game 1
Game 2
6
One Line Bingo
❶ ❷ ❸ ❹ ❺ ❻ ❼ ❽ ❾ ❿
Bingo

Homework Spot   `Track 71`

1 Look, listen and circle.

①  big  bib  pig
②  dish 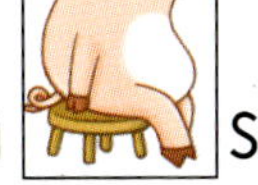 sit 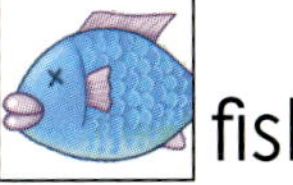 fish

③  wig 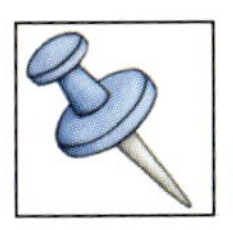 pin  win
④  six  hit  win

2 Listen and write.

①    ②    ③ 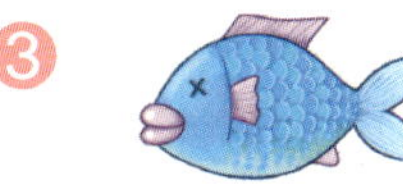   ④ 

____________   ____________   ____________   ____________

3 Listen and circle the correct word.

A big 

on the pig.

Fish on the 

. 

pigs 

the car.

4 Look, listen and circle.

Unit 11

The Short "o" Sound

10min

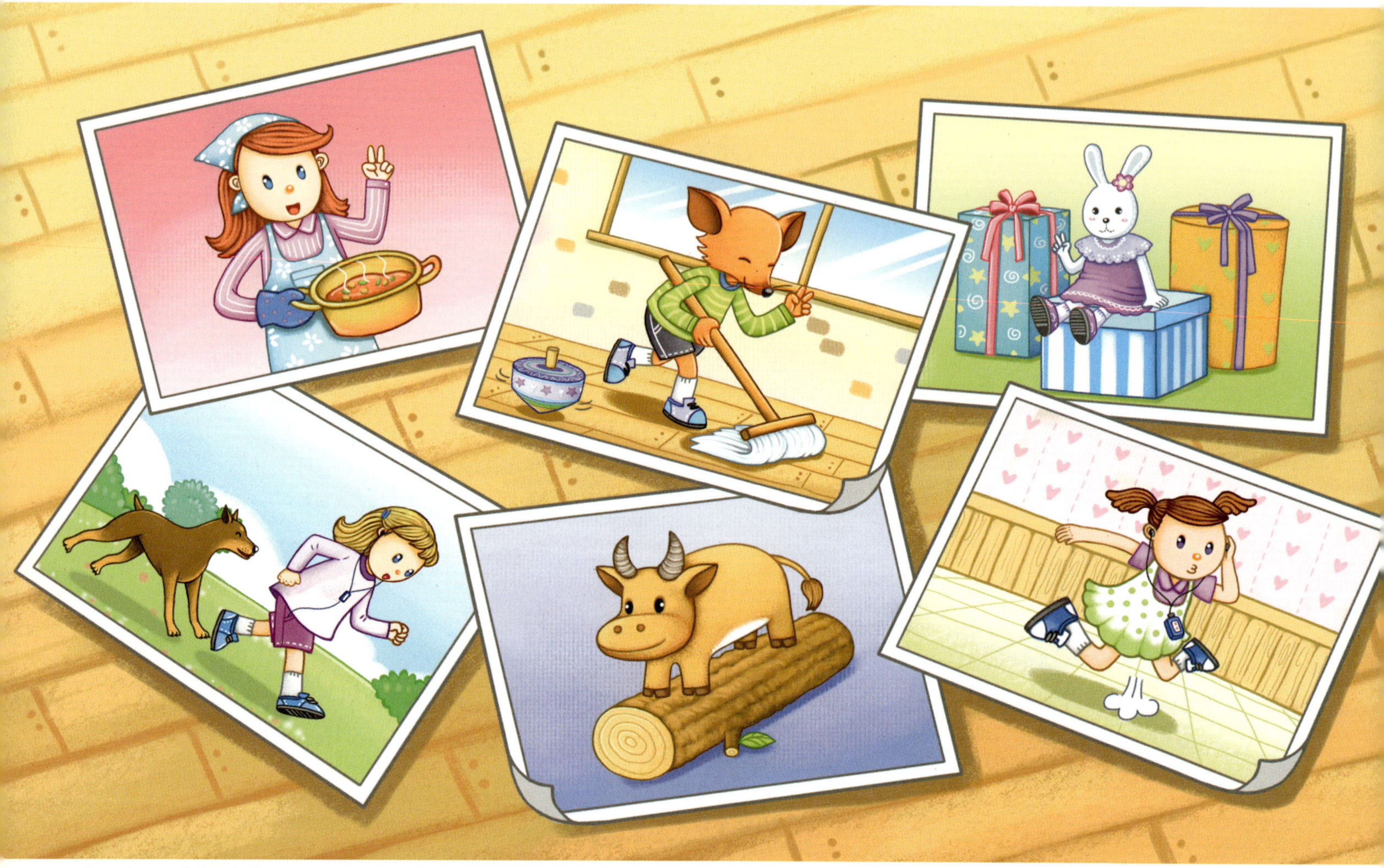

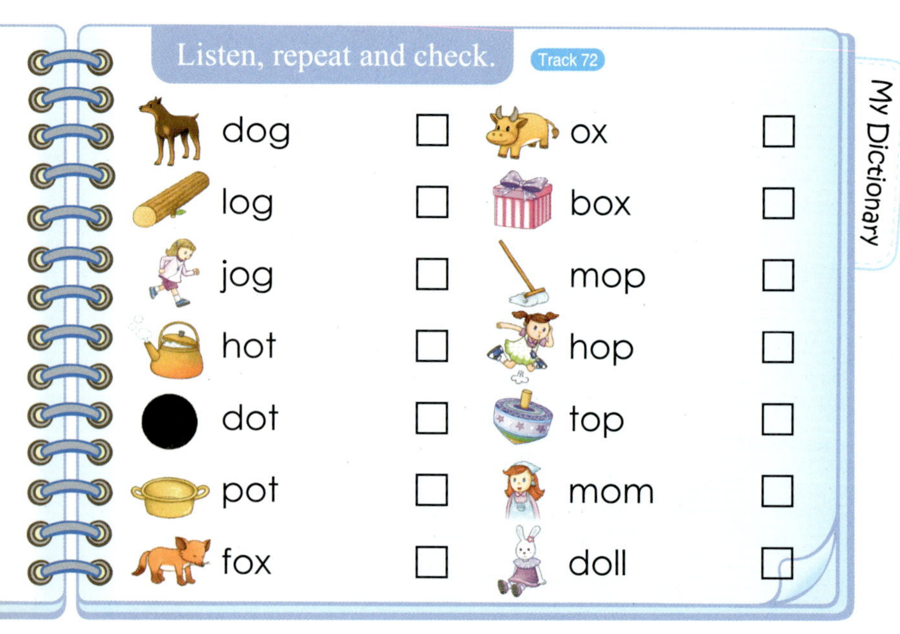

Look and find the new word, then circle.

Listen, repeat and check. Track 72

My Dictionary

dog	☐	ox	☐
log	☐	box	☐
jog	☐	mop	☐
hot	☐	hop	☐
dot	☐	top	☐
pot	☐	mom	☐
fox	☐	doll	☐

Listen and write. Track 73

1. f ____ x
2. t ____ p
3. d ____ t
4. j ____ g

 **Let's Chant**  10min

Listen and repeat. Track 74

Fox, box, Fox, box
A fox on the box.

Dog log, dog log
A dog hops on the log.

Mom, mop, mom, mop
Mom has a mop.

Hot pot, hot pot
The pot is hot.

POP QUIZ Fill in the blanks.

1. m _______

2. ___ o ___

3. d ______

4. ___ ot

5. b _____

6. ___ op

7. ___ o ___

8. ___ o ___ l

67

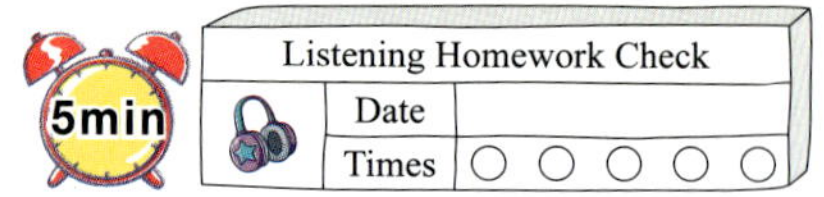

Listen and circle "Yes" if both have the same rhyming sound or "No" if not. Track 75

1. Yes — No   2. Yes — No   3. Yes — No

4. Yes — No   5. Yes — No   6. Yes — No

Listen and number. Match the picture to the correct word. Track 76

- dot

- top

- log

- hop

Mini Test Listen and write. Track 77

Score /5

1. _______ 2. _______ 3. _______ 4. _______ 5. _______

Circle the correct word and write. Then listen.  Track 78

On the log,

a _______ hops with a dog. fox   ox

The dog has a _______ . mop   top

The fox has a _______ . dot   pot

A box is on the _______ . fox   ox

A _______ is on the box. dot   hot

A _______ is on the box. pot   top

Circle the correct word.

1. dot
   hot
   pot

2. dog
   log
   jog

3. hop
   top
   mop

4. ox
   fox
   box

5. ox
   box
   fox

6. jog
   doll
   hog

Let's Play
Flick Flick
15min
Coins
Markers
How to play
① 각 칸에 short o 단어를 적습니다.
② 자신의 start 자리를 정하고 순서를 정한 뒤 자신의 땅을 칠할 색연필을 정합니다.
③ 검지로 동전을 튕겨서 위치하는 곳의 단어와 알파벳을 읽고 색칠하면 자신의 땅이 됩니다.
④ 모든 땅의 색이 칠해지면 칸의 개수가 많은 사람이 승리하게 됩니다.
Start
Start
One more space
Go back to start
+1
Start
Start
70

 **Homework Spot** Track 79

1 Listen and choose the correct word.

❶ dog log jog   ❷ hot pot dot   ❸ box fox ox

❹ hop mop top   ❺ mom doll mop

2 Listen and write the numbers in order.

3 Listen and circle the word.

A fox dog ox
on the box.

A dog hops on
the dog log box .

Mom has a
doll mop map .

The map pot bed
is hot.

4 Look, listen and circle.

The Short "u" Sound

10min

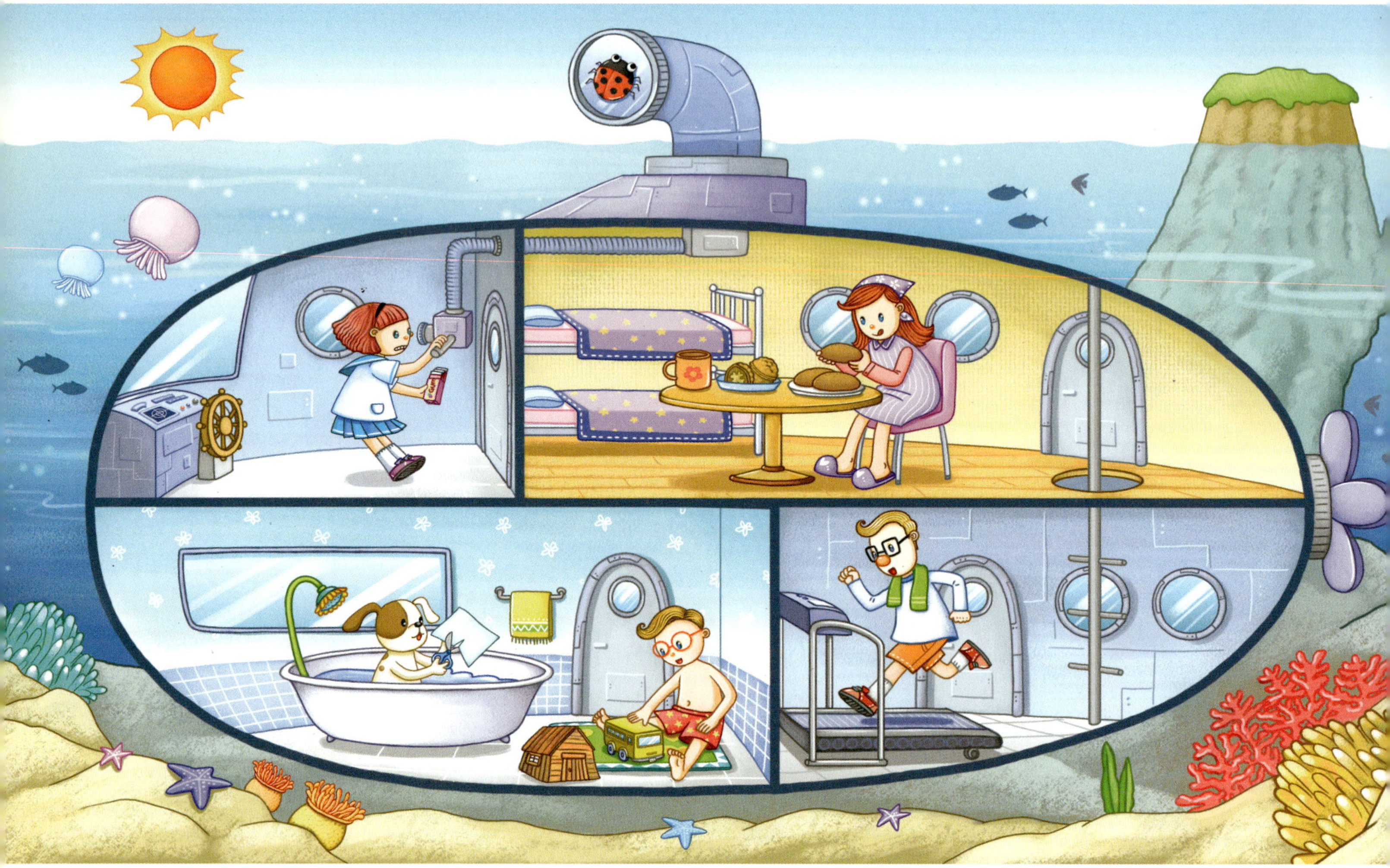

Look and find the new word, then circle.

Listen, repeat and check. Track 80

sun	☐	cup	☐	
run	☐	pup	☐	
bun	☐	gum	☐	
rug	☐	bus	☐	
bug	☐	cut	☐	
tub	☐	nut	☐	
sub	☐	hut	☐	

My Dictionary

Listen and write. Track 81

① s _____ n

② b _____ g

③ b _____ n

④ n _____ t

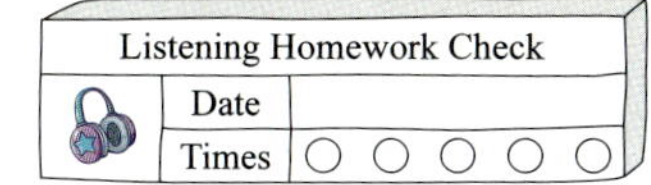

L isten and repeat. Track 82

Run, sun, run, sun
Run under the sun.

Bug, cup, bug, cup
A bug in the cup.

Pup, tub, pup, tub
A pup in the tub.

Nut, hut, nut, hut
A nut in the hut.

POP QUIZ Fill in the blanks.

73

Listen and circle, then write. Track 83

5min

1. 

p b u s g

2.

c d u t m

3.

t n g u b

4.

r c u g p

5.

b u s g t

6.

b u n g s

Listen, number and read. Track 84

nut

sun

pup

cup

run

hut

sub

gum

Mini Test Listen and write. Track 85

Score
/ 5

1. ________ 2. ________ 3. ________ 4. ________ 5. ________

Circle the correct word and write. Then listen.  Track 86 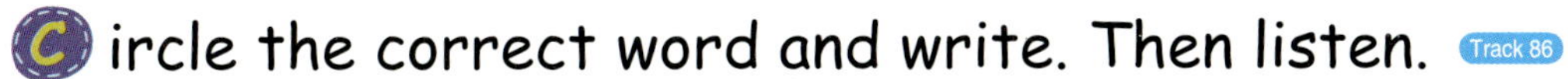

A pup has a ______ . rug cup

A ______ is in the cup. bug ham

The pup ______ fast. cap runs

The ______ runs in the cup. bug bat

We are in the ______ . bus bug

Here is a ______ . cup bun

Here is ______ . jam gum

______ a bun and gum. Cut Run

Complete the crossword puzzle.

1. s

2. u

3. n

4. t

5. u

6. p

Let's Play
Robot creation
15min
Coins
Paper clip
How to play
주사위를 던져 Start에서 출발합니다.
CHANCE칸에서는 동그란 보드판에 연필로 중심점에 클립을 고정시킨 뒤 클립을 손가락으로 퉁겨 나오는 수에 따라 움직입니다. "1st" – 현재 일등인 사람의 말 한 칸 앞으로, "Last" – 마지막 사람의 말 한 칸 뒤로 갑니다.
가장 먼저 Finish에 도착한 사람이 승리합니다.
Start
run
rug
CHANCE
bug
Finish
sun
cup
sub
tub
hut
sun
hut
CHANCE
cut
rug
run
gum
bun
bus
tub
rug
nut
gum
CHANCE
hut
pup
bug
rug
nut
1
2
5
1st
2
Last
cup
bug
cup
sub
sun
tub
CHANCE

Homework Spot `Track 87`

1 Listen and choose ✔ if they are same rhyming words or ✗ if not.

① ✔ ✗   ② ✔ ✗   ③ ✔ ✗   ④ ✔ ✗

2 Listen and circle. Then write.

①     ②     ③     ④  

_________________   _________________   _________________   _________________

3 Listen and choose the letter. Then write.

① 

b
n u
s
m

____

② 

p c s
u p

____

③ 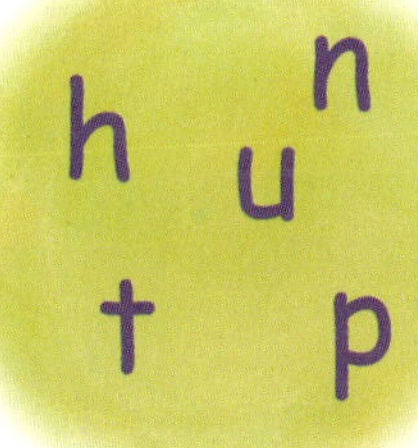

h n
u
t p

____

4 Listen, read and write the word from the word box.

A  _____________ has a  _____________ .

The  _____________ runs in the  _____________ .

 _____________ a  _____________ and  _____________ .

Word Box   pup gum cup bun cut bug

Unit 1

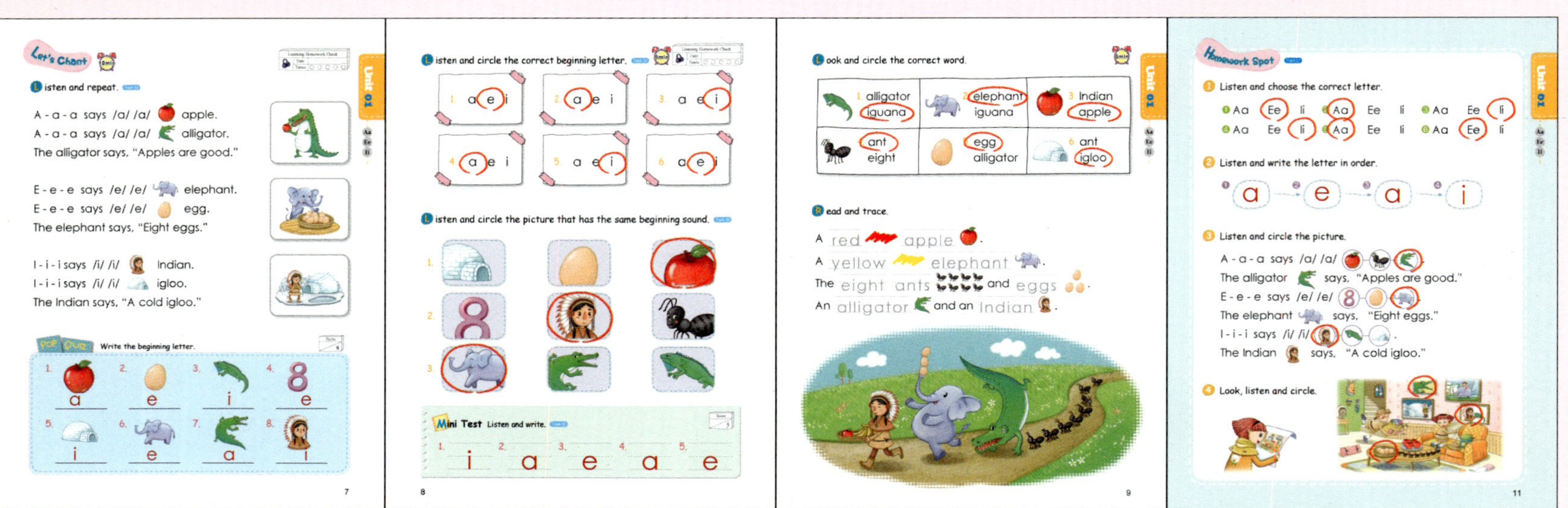

Unit 2

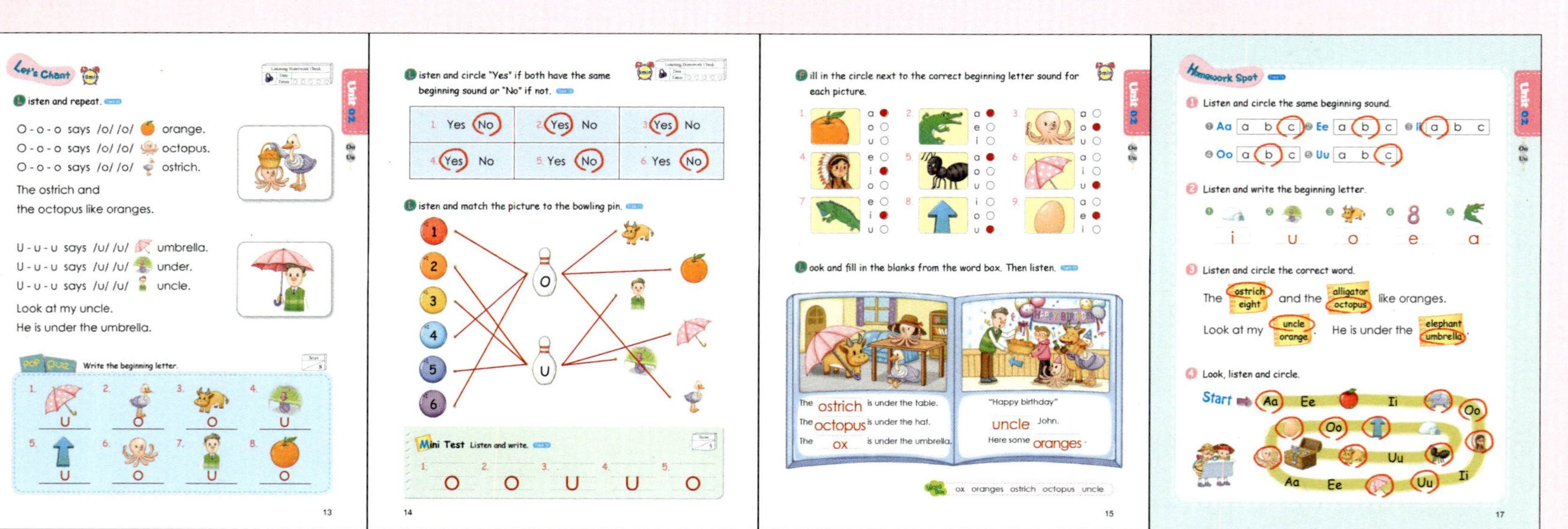

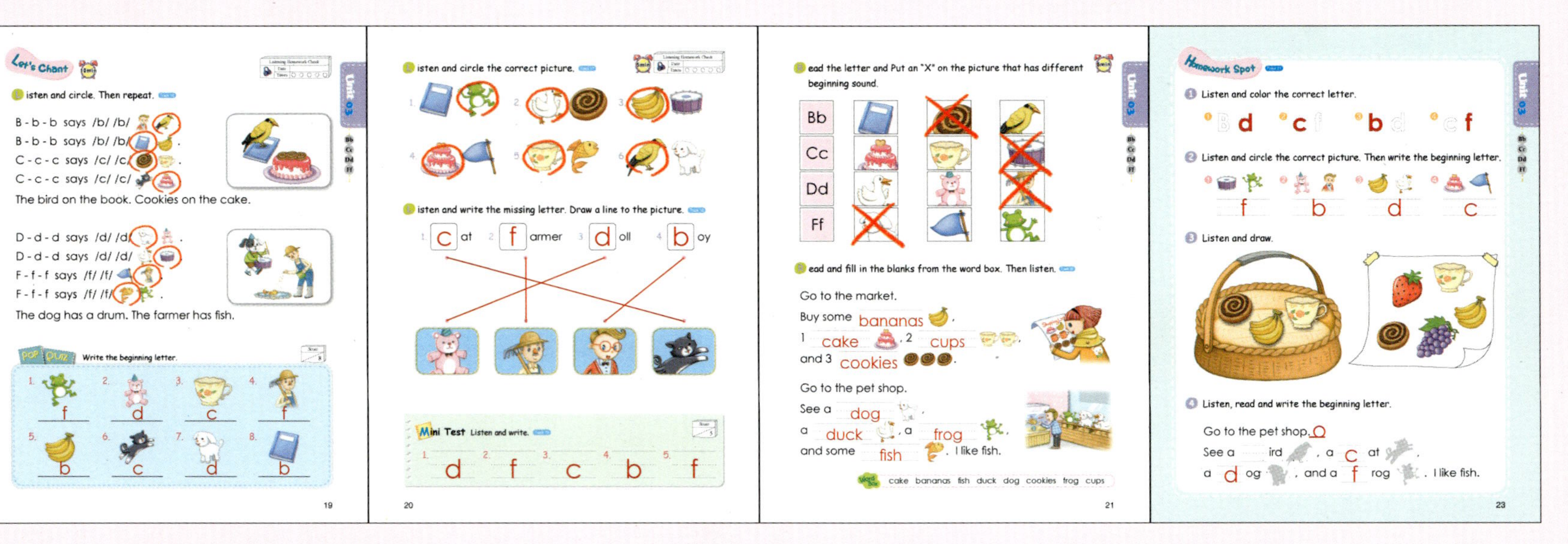

Unit 3

Let's Chant — Listen and circle. Then repeat.

B - b - b says /b/ /b/
B - b - b says /b/ /b/
C - c - c says /c/ /c/
C - c - c says /c/ /c/
The bird on the book. Cookies on the cake.

D - d - d says /d/ /d/
D - d - d says /d/ /d/
F - f - f says /f/ /f/
F - f - f says /f/ /f/
The dog has a drum. The farmer has fish.

POP QUIZ Write the beginning letter.
1. f 2. d 3. c 4. f
5. b 6. c 7. d 8. b

Listen and circle the correct picture.

Listen and write the missing letter. Draw a line to the picture.
1. c at 2. f armer 3. d oll 4. b oy

Mini Test Listen and write.
1. d 2. f 3. c 4. b 5. f

Read the letter and Put an "X" on the picture that has different beginning sound.

Bb
Cc
Dd
Ff

Read and fill in the blanks from the word box. Then listen.
Go to the market.
Buy some bananas.
1 cake, 2 cups
and 3 cookies.

Go to the pet shop.
See a dog.
a duck, a frog
and some fish. I like fish.

cake bananas fish duck dog cookies frog cups

Homework Spot
1. Listen and color the correct letter.
d c b f
2. Listen and circle the correct picture. Then write the beginning letter.
f b d c
3. Listen and draw.
4. Listen, read and write the beginning letter.
Go to the pet shop.
See a ird, a C at
a d og, and a f rog. I like fish.

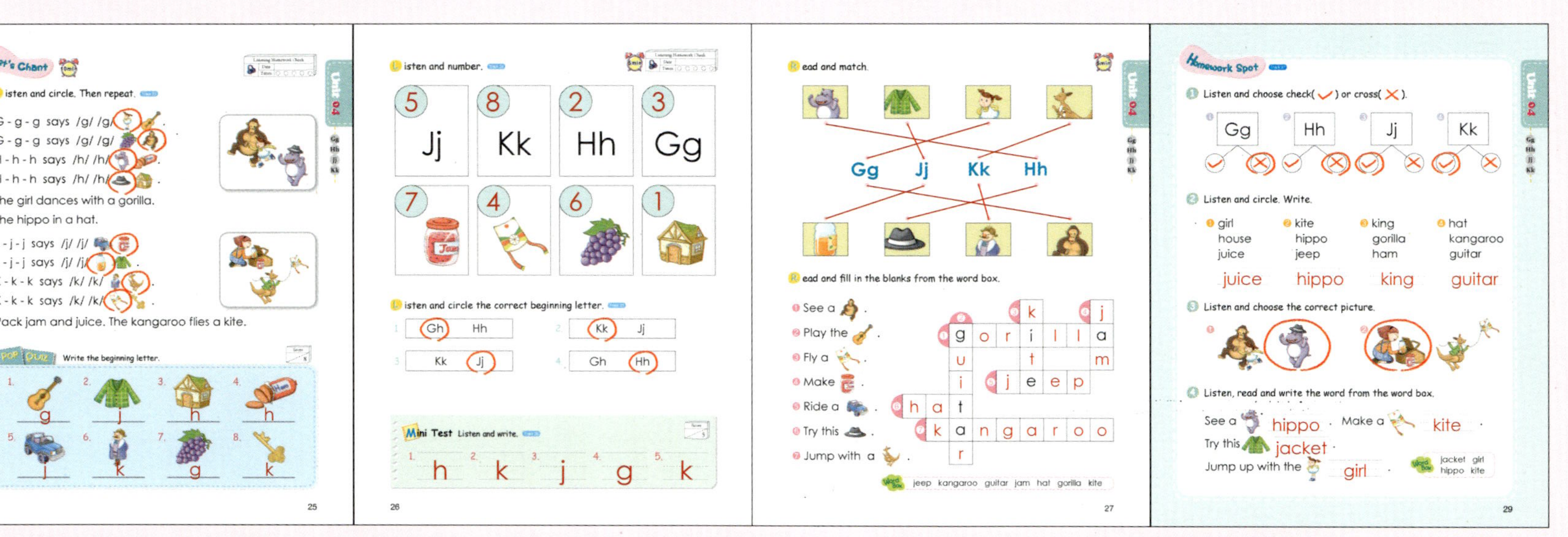

Unit 4

Let's Chant — Listen and circle. Then repeat.

G - g - g says /g/ /g/
G - g - g says /g/ /g/
H - h - h says /h/ /h/
H - h - h says /h/ /h/
The girl dances with a gorilla.
The hippo in a hat.

J - j - j says /j/ /j/
J - j - j says /j/ /j/
K - k - k says /k/ /k/
K - k - k says /k/ /k/
Pack jam and juice. The kangaroo flies a kite.

POP QUIZ Write the beginning letter.
1. g 2. h 3. h 4. h
5. j 6. k 7. g 8. k

Listen and number.
5 Jj 8 Kk 2 Hh 3 Gg
7 4 6 1

Listen and circle the correct beginning letter.
1. Gh / Hh 2. Kk / Jj
3. Kk / Jj 4. Gh / Hh

Mini Test Listen and write.
1. h 2. k 3. j 4. g 5. k

Read and match.
Gg Jj Kk Hh

Read and fill in the blanks from the word box.
1. See a
2. Play the
3. Fly a
4. Make
5. Ride a
6. Try this
7. Jump with a

gorilla, a, t, m, u, i, jeep, h a t, k a n g a r o o, r, k, j

jeep kangaroo guitar jam hat gorilla kite

Homework Spot
1. Listen and choose check(✓) or cross(✗).
Gg Hh Jj Kk
2. Listen and circle. Write.
girl / house / juice → juice
kite / hippo / jeep → hippo
king / gorilla / ham → king
hat / kangaroo / guitar → guitar
3. Listen and choose the correct picture.
4. Listen, read and write the word from the word box.
See a hippo. Make a kite.
Try this jacket.
Jump up with the girl.

jacket girl
hippo kite

Unit 5

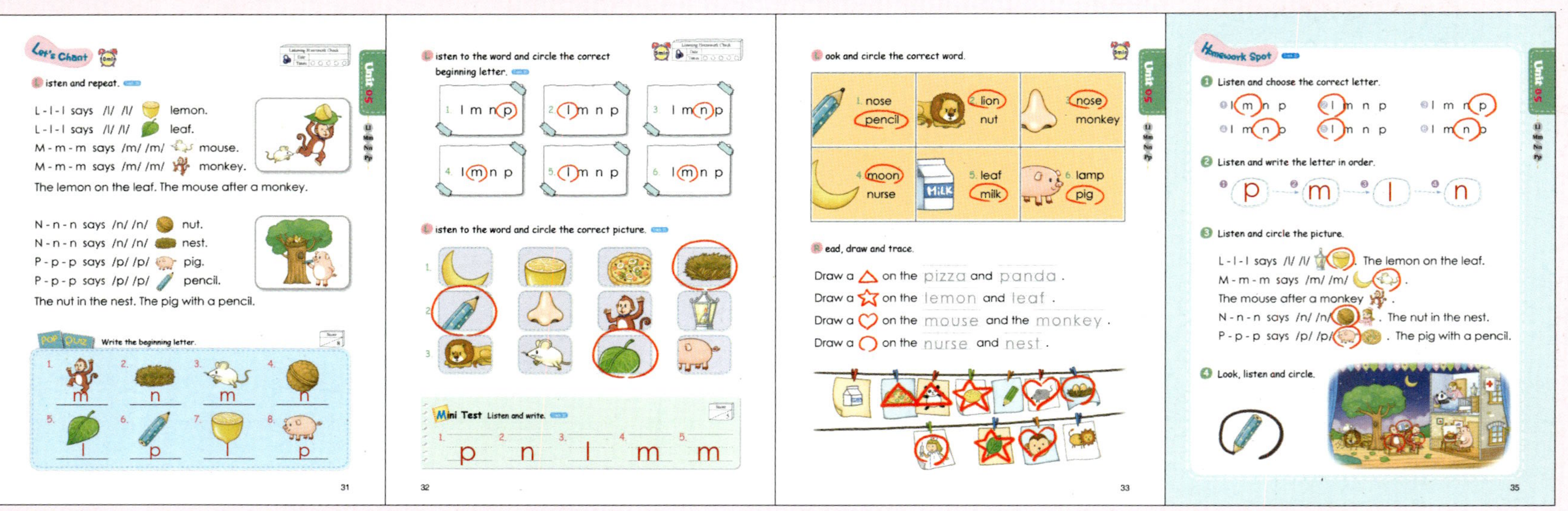

Unit 6

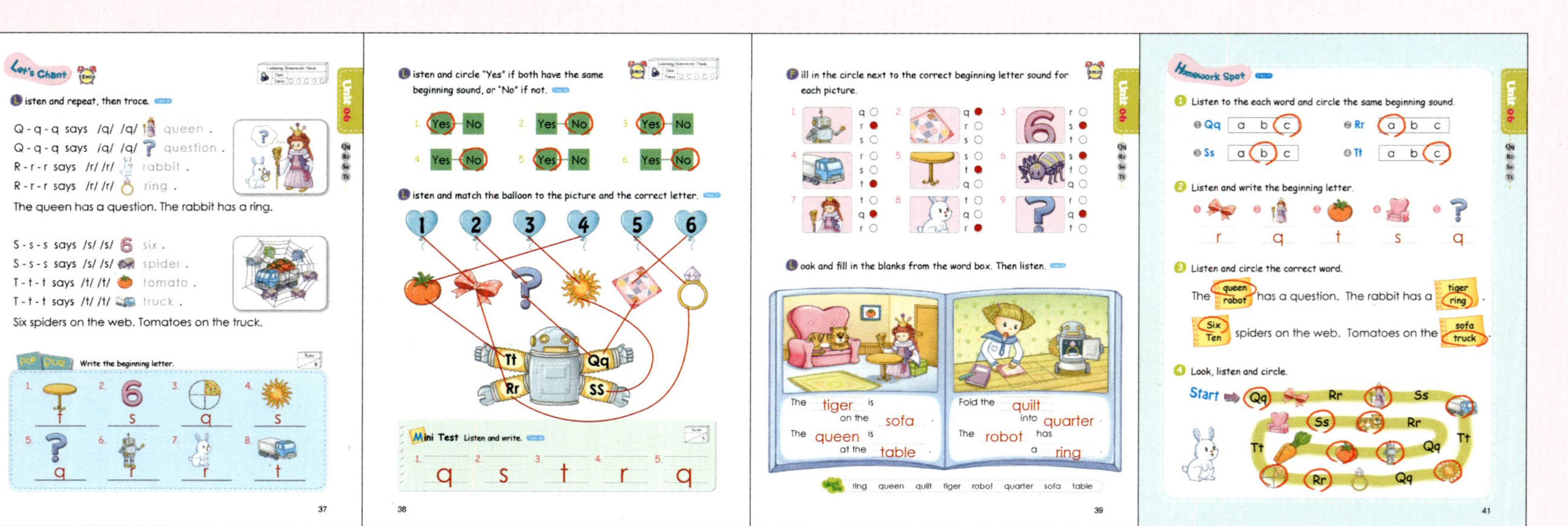

Unit 7

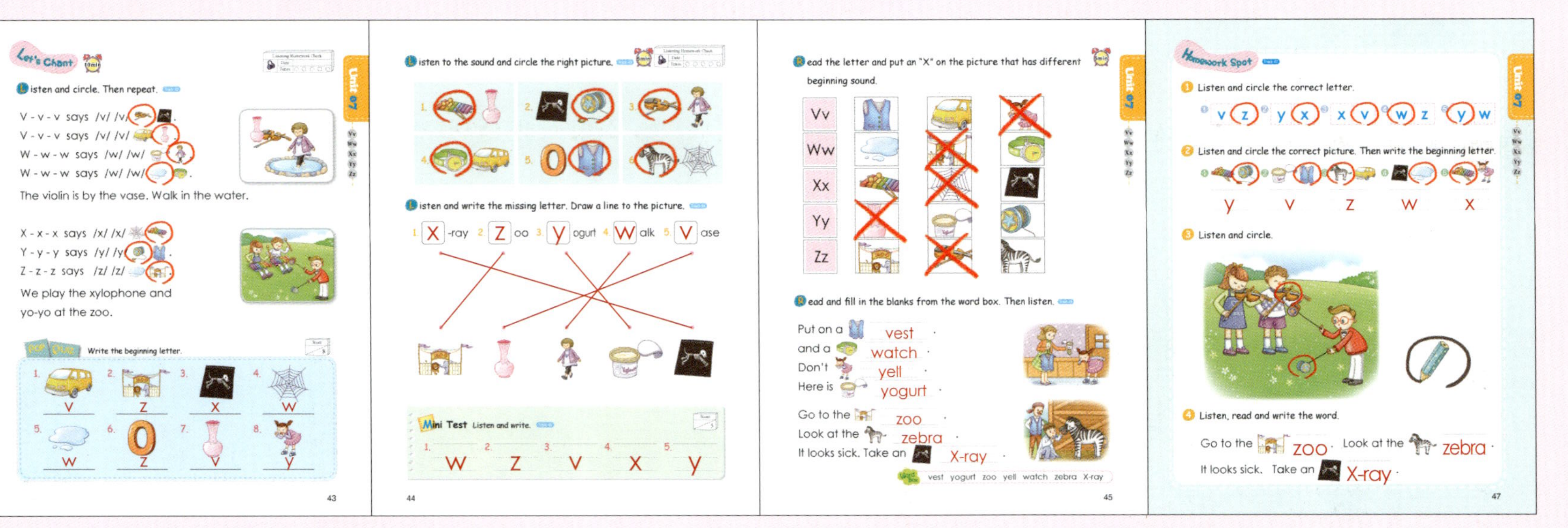
Let's Chant
Listen and circle. Then repeat.
V - v - v says /v/ /v/
V - v - v says /v/ /v/
W - w - w says /w/ /w/
W - w - w says /w/ /w/
The violin is by the vase. Walk in the water.
X - x - x says /x/ /x/
Y - y - y says /y/ /y/
Z - z - z says /z/ /z/
We play the xylophone and yo-yo at the zoo.
Write the beginning letter.
1. v 2. z 3. x 4. w
5. w 6. z 7. v 8. y
43
Listen to the sound and circle the right picture.
Listen and write the missing letter. Draw a line to the picture.
1. X-ray 2. Z oo 3. Y ogurt 4. W alk 5. V ase
Mini Test Listen and write.
1. w 2. z 3. v 4. x 5. y
44
Read the letter and put an "X" on the picture that has different beginning sound.
Vv Ww Xx Yy Zz
Read and fill in the blanks from the word box. Then listen.
Put on a vest
and a watch
Don't yell
Here is yogurt
Go to the zoo
Look at the zebra
It looks sick. Take an X-ray
vest yogurt zoo yell watch zebra X-ray
45
Homework Spot
1. Listen and circle the correct letter.
v z y x x v w z y w
2. Listen and circle the correct picture. Then write the beginning letter.
y v z w x
3. Listen and circle.
4. Listen, read and write the word.
Go to the zoo . Look at the zebra .
It looks sick. Take an X-ray .
47

Unit 8

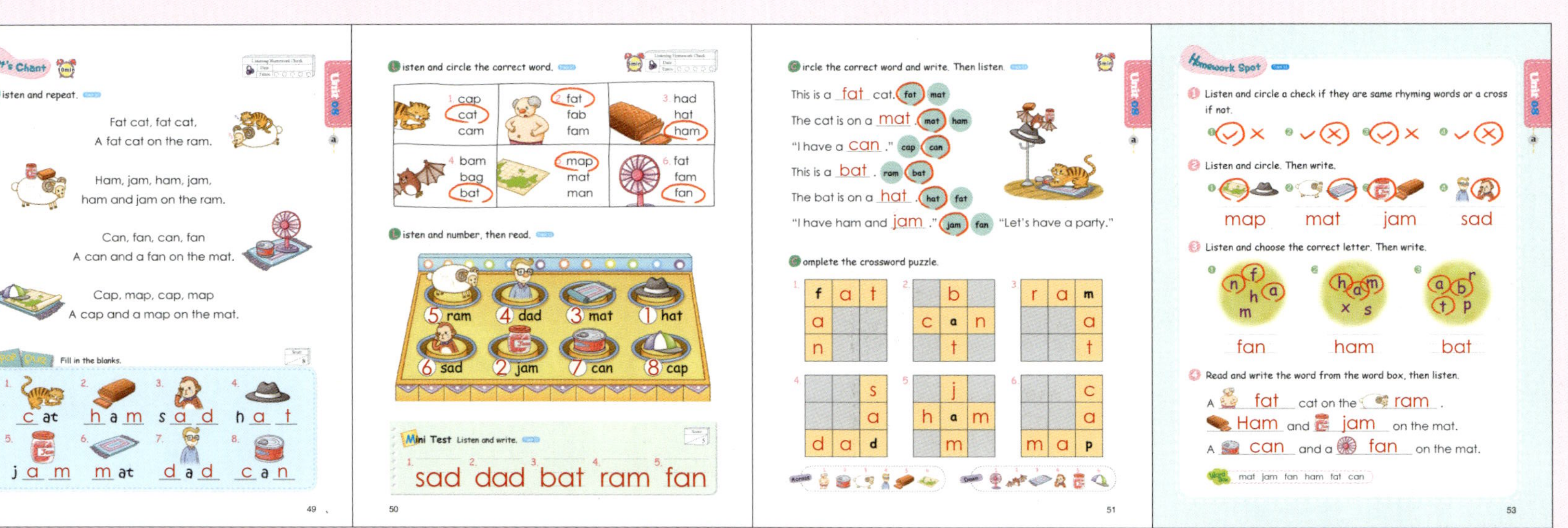
Let's Chant
Listen and repeat.
Fat cat, fat cat,
A fat cat on the ram.
Ham, jam, ham, jam,
ham and jam on the ram.
Can, fan, can, fan
A can and a fan on the mat.
Cap, map, cap, map
A cap and a map on the mat.
Fill in the blanks.
1. c at 2. h am 3. s ad 4. h at
5. j am 6. m at 7. d ad 8. c an
49
Listen and circle the correct word.
1. cap cat cam 2. fat fab fam 3. had hat ham
4. bam bag bat 5. map mat man 6. fat fam fan
Listen and number, then read.
5. ram 4. dad 3. mat 1. hat
6. sad 2. jam 7. can 8. cap
Mini Test Listen and write.
sad dad bat ram fan
50
Circle the correct word and write. Then listen.
This is a fat cat. fat mat
The cat is on a mat . mat ham
"I have a can ." cap can
This is a bat . ram bat
The bat is on a hat . hat fat
"I have ham and jam ." jam fan "Let's have a party."
Complete the crossword puzzle.
f a t   b   r a m
a   c a n   a
n   t   t
     s   j   c
     a   h a m   a
d a d   m   m a p
51
Homework Spot
1. Listen and circle a check if they are same rhyming words or a cross if not.
2. Listen and circle. Then write.
map mat jam sad
3. Listen and choose the correct letter. Then write.
fan ham bat
4. Read and write the word from the word box, then listen.
A fat cat on the ram .
Ham and jam on the mat.
A can and a fan on the mat.
mat jam fan ham fat can
53

Answer

Answer

Unit 9

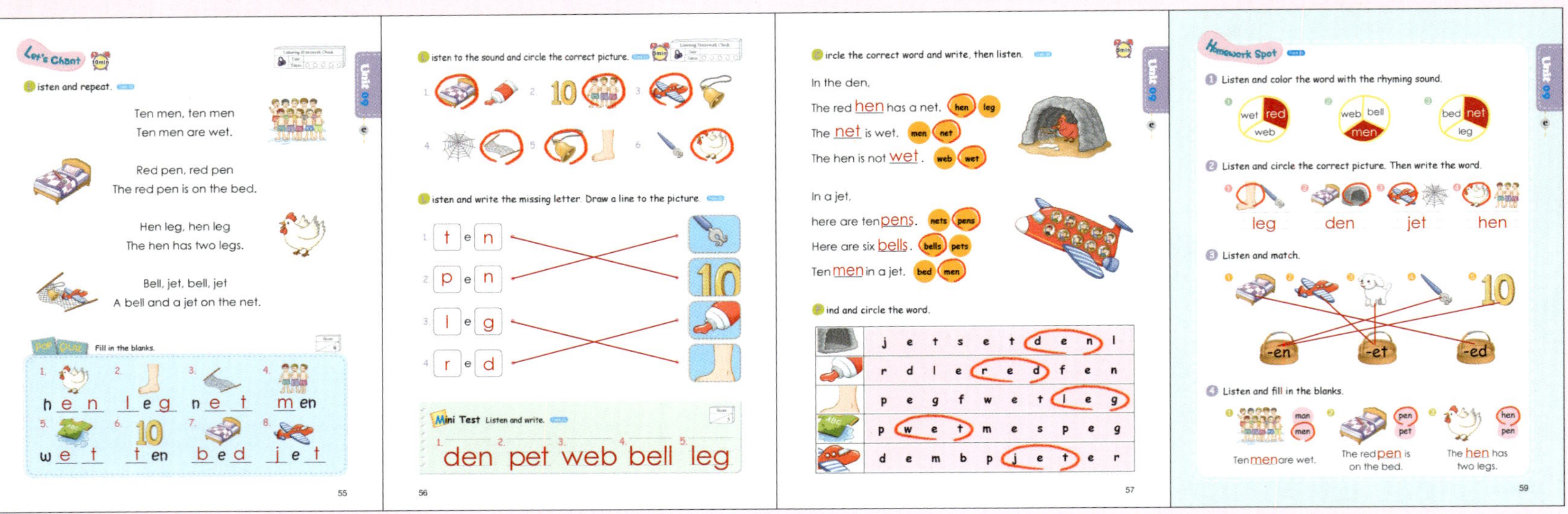

Unit 10

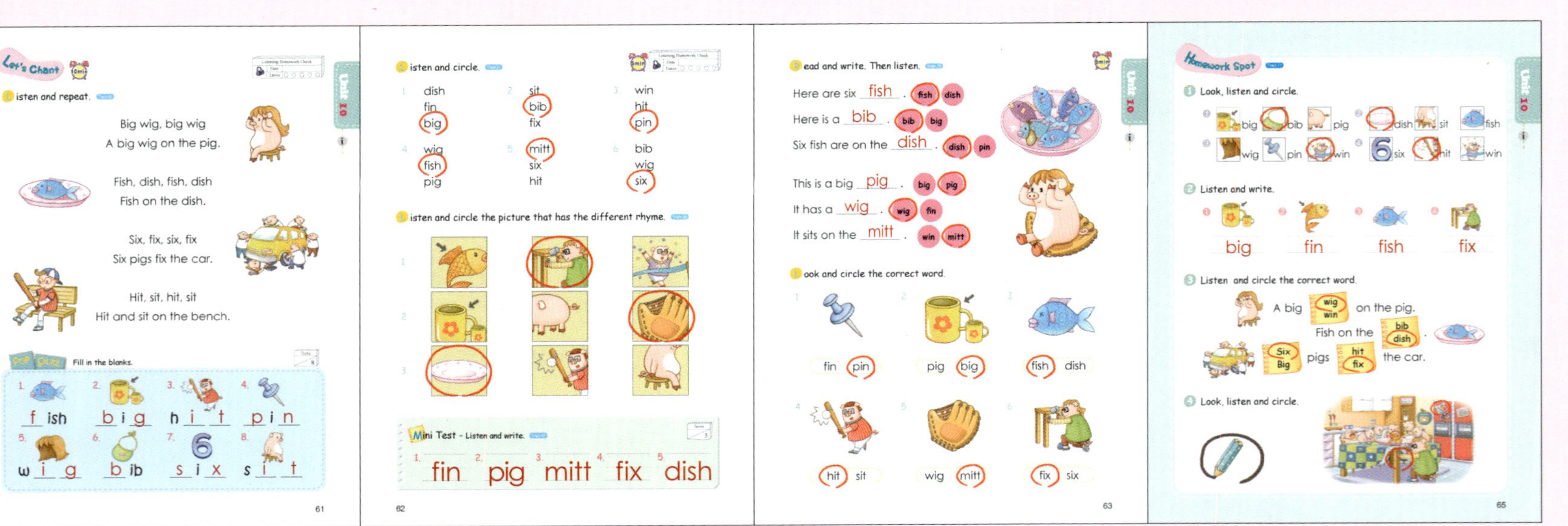

Unit 11

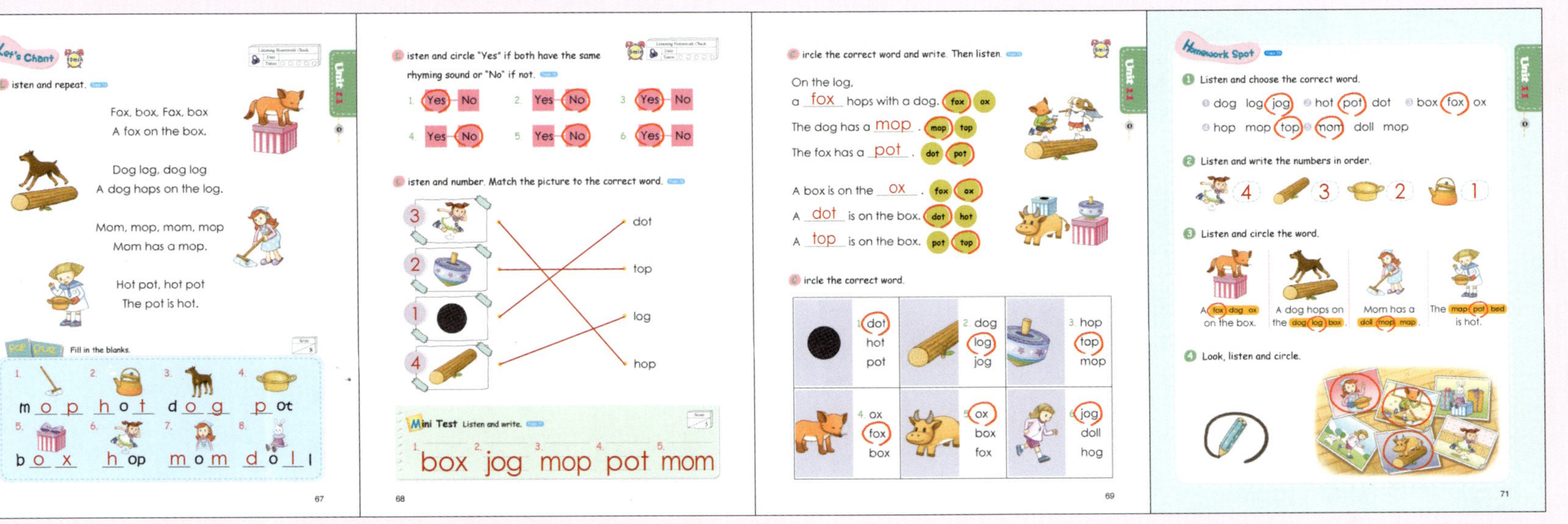

Unit 12

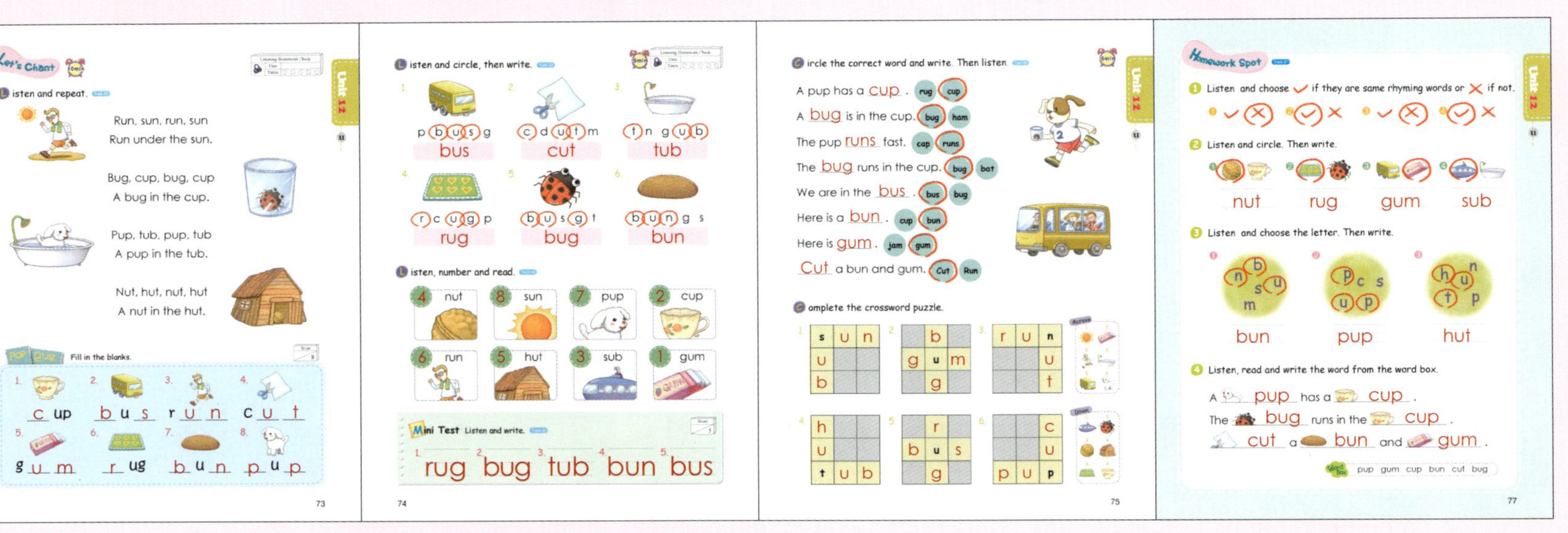

 Index

 alligator	 box	 cut
 ant	 boy	 dad
 apple	 bug	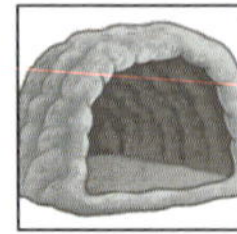 den
 banana	 bun	 dish
 bat	 bus	 dog
 bed	 cake	 doll
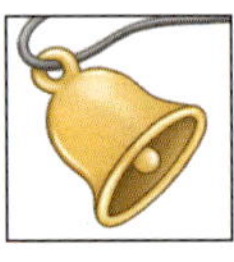 bell	 can	 dot
 bib	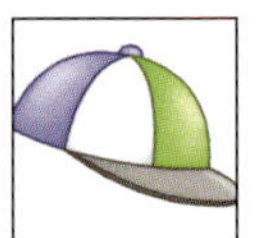 cap	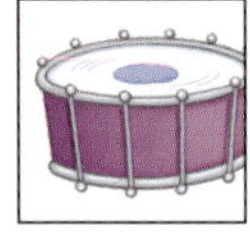 drum
 big	 cat	 duck
 bird	 cookie	 egg
 book	 cup	 eight

elephant	gorilla	house
fan	grapes	hut
farmer	guitar	igloo
fat	gum	iguana
fin	ham	Indian
fish	hat	jacket
fix	hen	jam
flag	hippo	jeep
fox	hit	jet
frog	hop	jog
girl	hot	juice

 kangaroo

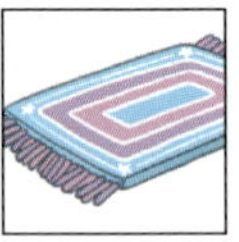 mat

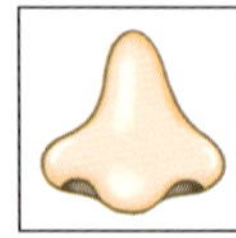 nose

 key

 men

 nurse

 king

 milk

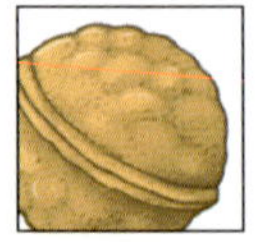 nut

 kite

 mitt

 octopus

 lamp

 mom

 orange

 leaf

 monkey

 ostrich

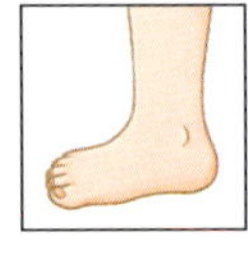 leg

 moon

 ox

 lemon

 mop

 panda

 lion

 mouse

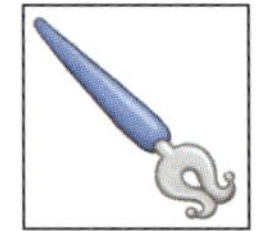 pen

 log

 nest

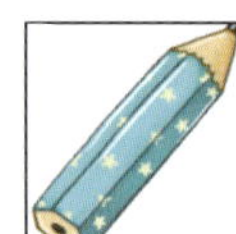 pencil

 map

 net

 pet

 pig

 pin

 pizza

 pot

 pup

 quarter

 queen

question

quilt

rabbit

ram

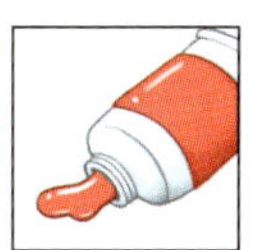 red

 ribbon

 ring

 robot

 rug

 run

 sad

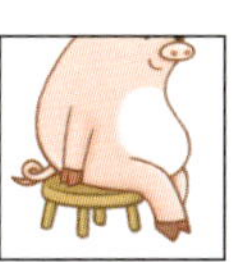 sit

 six

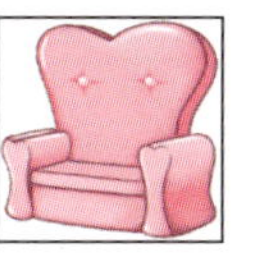 sofa

 spider

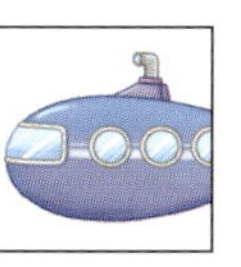 sub

 sun

 table

 ten

 tiger

 tomato

 top

 truck

 tub

 umbrella

 uncle

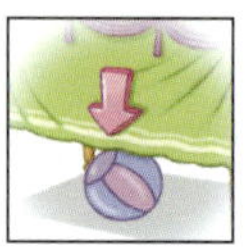 under

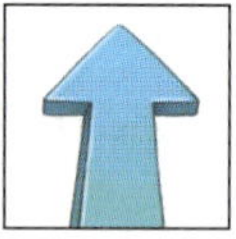 up

 van

 vase

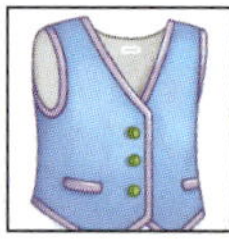 vest

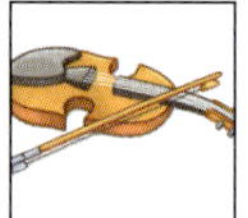 violin

 walk

 watch

 water

 web

 wet

 wig

 win

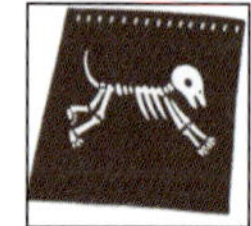 X-ray

 xylophone

 yell

 yogurt

 yo-yo

 zebra

 zero

 zoo

Publication	2011.04.15

Author	Joy Park
Supervisor	LittleLambSchool English Research Institute
Illustration	Joohi Jeong
Publisher	KiSeon Lee
Publishing Company	JPlus Publishing Co.
Address	467-30 Mangwon-dong, Mapo-gu, Seoul 121-826, Korea
Telephone	02-332-8320, 02-3142-2520
Fax	02-332-8321
Web site	www.jplus114.com
Registration Number	10-1680
Registration Date	1998. 12. 09
ISBN	978-89-92215-68-8